C000252993

Upt

Audrey Macnaughton

**Dogs Life
Books**

Published in 2021 by Dogs Life Books

Copyright © Audrey Macnaughton 2021

Audrey Macnaughton has asserted her right to be identified as the
author of this Work in accordance with the Copyright, Designs and
Patents Act 1988

ISBN Paperback: 978-1-9196443-0-1
Ebook: 978-1-9196443-1-8

A CIP catalogue copy of this book can be found in the British Library.

Published with the help of Indie Authors World
www.indieauthorsworld.com

IndieAuthors
World

This book is dedicated to my dad. The ultimate storyteller and observer of the hilarity of life.

I miss you every single day.

Audrey x

Acknowledgements

Thank you to my brilliant sons. There is always something to jot down with you two around, mainly because I want to cherish every moment I have with you. You continue to give me so many proud moments and laughs that make any situation better. You've also given me worry lines, so I can blame you, thank you.

Thank you to Shaun, my partner in grime. You are a phenomenal support and I couldn't do all the things I get up to without you. I don't mean it when I get grumpy (yeah I actually do!).

Writing stuff down is fun, wrestling it into a book is hard. Thank you to Michael Heppell for all your help on your *Write that Book Masterclass*. I joined thinking I could "skulk at the back" but your challenges and shoves along the way kept me going. And here you are, an actual book.

My working group on the Masterclass are all amazing authors. They are creative, inspirational and just the right side of pushy. Thank you for supporting me, giving me ideas and putting up with the odd tear.

Everyone at Indie Authors World has been so generous with their time, feedback and expertise. You've taken my book from a manuscript to a thing of pride.

Finally.

My family and I got through 2020 and many did not. My thoughts remain with every single person who has lost their life to this awful virus. Thank you to everyone who has worked tirelessly to bring care to people, at the most difficult and frightening of times. You stepped into the fray every day and are still doing it. Your dedication and humanity is incredible. Thank you.

Introduction

About Me

I'm nobody special. Just a Mum of two boys, who runs a business and tries to laugh more and drink less. I fail at the drinking less, as you will read in this book.

I'm not a key worker, not a big important businesswoman and neither me nor any of my family got COVID (yet, touch wood.) But I chronicled the 100 days of the first UK lockdown and this book is a gallop through the roller coaster of family life.

Journaling

I'm an avid journaler and do all my scribbling in little notebooks from Smythson the stationers. I try my hand at drawing (inadequately and with often hilarious results) but most of all I try to capture the small stuff, the everyday detail that disappears from our memory.

About the Gang

I live with lots of chaps! There are my two teenage sons, James and Archie, my partner Shaun and our two whippet dogs, Arthur and Spike.

The final one in the line-up is Sheldon the cat (Shelly for short). He looks lovely and fluffy but he is murderous.

You'll get an idea of his temperament if I tell you that when people go to stroke him, we all shout "oh god, don't touch him!" He's a black ball of badness, but he's ours and he concludes the gang known as the Gosforth Fam.

Week 1

Day 1: Monday 23rd March

We are now in full isolation which is one step away from lockdown. The Government command (moved on from suggestion) is that everyone who can, stays at home. No visits, no gathering in groups, even outside. You are only allowed out for essentials such as food and medicine.

I nip to the office to change the answer machine message, pick up some files and generally check the place over.

I then nip - lots of nipping which makes a change from popping! Maybe nipping is more apt when you're not following the advice to the letter and you're trying to be stealthy? Anyway, I nip to Lidl and manage to procure some essentials. This included coffee beans and pain-au-chocolat for the boys' breakfast. First world problems right there in that single sentence.

There was still no toilet roll to be had. This emerging crisis has had twists and turns already but the panic buying, and resultant shortage of toilet roll has to be the most prolonged, weird and annoying.

All I seem to have ended up stockpiling has been cheese!

Prior to the shop closures we did the M&S dine in for two with cheese. I then happened to be in town when Fenwicks was closing so I went into the foodhall and got a huge piece of stilton for £2.

Bloody marvellous and I figured it was a lot better than toilet roll. Although if this drags on I may regret my choice of stockpiling item.

After all my "nipping" I get the boys up for breakfast. Wow that's hard without the deadline of the "get in the sodding car" screech for the school run.

Archie says he is tired and, it has to be said, is a reluctant participant in the school distance learning. But he eventually disappears into the Devil's Room (our name for the strange little room off the kitchen which has a desk, computer, printer, bookshelves and unhelpfully the cat litter tray along with a few air fresheners – it's a heady mix).

As he drags his feet, I'm minded that this is a great move forward from his comment on Saturday which went something like this: "Can one of you fellas sign into the online lessons for me on Monday? It means that I can lie in bed and you'll feel that you're being helpful! You'll kill two birds with one stone."

Eh?

It got even funnier when he followed up with "what does kill two birds with one stone even mean?"

Suffice to say we didn't entertain his request of being helpful and he's ready with his headphones clamped on to listen in to his lessons. I reckon that will be his "look" for the duration of this 12 weeks.

I forgot to say that bit didn't I? 12 weeks is the length of time now being hinted at by the Government and wheeled out in the press. 12 weeks or as it will become known "12 bloody weeks!"

Day 2: Tuesday 24th March

It's all got a lot more real now. We watched the Prime Minister's news announcement last night – the press gatherings have been changed to just Johnson on his own telling us what we are to do. I refuse to call him Boris or any other term of endearment as he has a job to do and we need to treat him like a grown up.

Last night the message was that we must stay at home and we're only allowed out for one piece of exercise per day.

No loitering in parks or chatting to neighbours while on a dog walk. Park benches are taped off to stop us from being tempted into a little loiter, and playgrounds are out of bounds.

You are still allowed out for essentials but now if you are to go to the supermarket, you must go on your own and observe the social distancing of two metres apart.

Walking the dogs is a nightmare. It's bloody rush hour on the bloody bridlepath. There's the usual dogwalkers but also people trying to tire out toddlers and with the gyms all closed people are now jogging or cycling in the great outdoors. People on the bridlepath fall into three main categories:

First, there are normal people like us who keep a distance, wait for others to pass and generally still smile and say hello. It's funny how when you describe groups of people you always put yourself into the "normal" group. The level-headed group where everyone does the "right" thing. Yeah, that's my group, obvs.

The second category is the people who have been displaced from the gyms. They seem to still think that they are on a running machine or are in some sort of virtual reality game. Either way, we don't exist and they just cut through and ignore everyone. They certainly don't bother saying thank you when you wait for them at narrow parts of the path. Rude.

I try to stop my chuntering annoyance by remembering that they are in a complete world of their own, perhaps used to being in a gym with headphones on and with the express task of avoiding eye contact with anyone. Gyms can be like that.

Finally, the nervous ones who are in full panic mode. When our paths cross, they dive into the side looking terror stricken while grabbing their children. I have two things to say to them:

1. I am not a zombie
2. Go home if you're so terrified! You're stressing me out and your child looks catatonic.

I'm pretty sure "stranger danger" is going to be at a whole new level now.

Onto the next consideration of this "all being at home existence". I realise that everyone doing individual grazing when they are hungry isn't going to work. We'd all eat at different times, we would run out of key ingredients such as bread, and I wouldn't be able to monitor/curtail the incidents of "Mum can I have a snack?", followed at mealtimes by the equally unhelpful phrase "oh I'm not that hungry just now".

So, I've opened the "Gosforth Fam Café".

As a café it's convivial but it has defined opening times and strict rules on what are approved snacks and refreshments outside of the normal hours.

I started doing my poster yesterday and when I put down breakfast opening times as 8am – 9am there was a near riot from the clientele. The negotiations started, so I immediately changed the hours to 8am – 8:50am. Those boys never learn that this is how Mum negotiates.

The approved snacks during the day are fruit and veg sticks but I had to clarify that Coca-Cola wasn't on the drinks list.

"But what about pudding or snacks in front of a film?" is the next issue. Lord, it would be easier to negotiate Brexit than have to go head-to-head with these two! We opt for a dessert slot 7pm – 8pm to cover TV snackage and I set about doing some drawings to make the poster look good. James said it was missing one drawing and simulated sketching out a swastika which I felt was a bit harsh!

The lunchtime regime was followed by the dinnertime regime. I feel that this way of living is a bizarre combination of all-inclusive holiday and prison! But all in all, it's not too bad and actually quite nice. Don't think I will go back to the old ways – wonder how often I'll say that during this pandemic?

Day 3: Wednesday 25th March

I've taken the step of securing the breakfast orders the night before. I'm thinking of getting those things that you hang on your bedroom door in hotels, but for now it's a verbal order system.

This was mainly to curb the bacon and egg notion that I suspect may slip in as a habit. It's not the bloody 1950's!

Honestly, this whole near lockdown will be dominated by food shopping and menu planning. But the nice bit is that we are having all our meals together, chatting and also tackling the Disney jigsaw that I bought on Saturday.

Maybe we are in the 1950's!

I had a little food strop today. It started out as the usual banter from the chaps about bending the food rules and then it went a bit further with a quip from Shaun about the need for them to enjoy themselves.

Well yes, they can flipping enjoy themselves because I'm doing all the damn organising. That's not quite how I put it.

It was more of a full volume rant of "eat what you fudging well like whenever you fudging well want and then next week you'll starve as there will be no food in the supermarkets and I won't even care."

Something like that. But to find out just ask our neighbours because we were in our garden and they were just over the fence in full earshot of the tirade.

Nice! And this on Day 3.

"Audrey, come to the Diary Room!"

Day 4: Thursday 26th March

Porridge is the order again today, but mealtimes have changed. Reason being is that my poster got a bit damaged by a water spillage – yeah right, by accident was it, fellas?

The boys tried to turn the now missing words to their advantage by reading out their interpretation with statements such as "that now reads 'unlimited snacks'", "look no end time for breakfast". They also made a bit of an attempt at getting out of the chores – I haven't mentioned those have I? The "deal" with the café is that it only opens if the chores are done with no argy bargy!

Not wanting to be without my main bargaining chip, I had nipped into the office (note the nipped word again as it was probably against the rules) and had picked up a craft box so now the new poster has a foam lady superhero sticker with the caption "Keep Mum Sane" and other new items such as an empty box titled "Space for new rules if there are ANY arguments". Oh, and the much-needed clarification "Fudge is not fruit"!

So, I'm getting ready for breakfast at the new poster time of 8:15 – 8:45am with the added great news of the unveiling of a new orange juice that I'd hidden at the back of the fridge. These are the ration strategies that work with a group who are both gannets and unobservant.

It's another lovely day so I take the opportunity between emails and phone calls to get the dog beds washed and out on the washing line. Small but important sense of achievement was the result! Similar feeling to the one yesterday when I cleaned the windows. I'm aiming to get a bigger house chore done each day for two reasons.

Firstly, to get rid of my "work ethic energy" – I feel the change of pace is akin to zooming along on a motorway and suddenly being faced with really slow-moving traffic. You have a rising sense of anxiety and frustration to get moving.

Secondly, I hope the house starts to feel cleaner. You know when people say proudly "my house might be messy but it's clean", well I'm the opposite, it's tidy but utterly manky.

What, though, is the big event ahead of us today?

We're getting Disney Plus. Unlimited access to Disney films and programmes, everything Marvel and the item we used to persuade Shaun, National Geographic.

Just before tea, I take the dogs out for my single piece of exercise (Government rules) and the dogs second walk. Shaun does the morning one, so he is also sticking to the one piece of exercise. But the little whippets need two walks and have no truck with human laws anyway.

Pleasant walk through the wood and onto the golf course. Didn't see a soul until the return journey when I was met with the 5:30pm rush hour on the bloody bridlepath.

The usual dog walkers and also now a new contingent in a running troupe. The runners had set themselves up with a little route of sprints ending at the narrow bridge, for a relaxed little congregate.

What?! Really?! A group of people gathering?

I stop with the dogs and wait for them to bunch up a bit so I could walk past. Nope, they just stared at me as though I was some paranoid old biddy (perhaps I have slipped out of my "normal category"?). So, I just went "full busy-body" and walked past them and grumbled "WTF" pretty loudly. That's the way to deal with irresponsible behaviour in the youth, a good old bit of concealed aggressive behaviour at a safe (social) distance.

I get home and have a big gin. That's the other way to deal with this crisis although that does break the Gosforth Fam Café rule of no alcohol except Friday to Sunday.

Ah what the hell, I wrote the rules, and it is thirsty Thursday after all… chin chin!

Day 5: Friday 27ᵗʰ March

James and I are sneaking out to the office, but I have a story in case the police stop us.

That sounds like an exaggeration but in other parts of the country police are pulling cars over to check if people have a legitimate reason to be out of their homes. The valid reasons can be shopping for food, getting medicine or going to work in one of the few approved jobs which includes healthcare and teaching (although the schools are closed for most, they are still open for the children of key workers).

Despite a try by the owner Mike Ashley, Sports Direct is not considered a critical service and his heartfelt appeal that people had to exercise, was perhaps a bit tenuous and got rejected. Of course, this will end up being the bloody week that we find out the boys have grown out of their trainers won't it?!

I'm not a key worker despite spending all week helping clients navigate their staffing arrangements through the crisis including home working, related GDPR concerns, layoffs, sickness pay as well as the whole new world of furlough. All these words that we never used before. Furlough comes from an old piece of employment law to do with dockers at ports and it means you can temporarily lay off staff. It's now being bandied around "oh yes have you never furloughed", "we've always furloughed".

Anyway, despite all of these shenanigans, I'm not a key worker so must stay at home. But the story to the police is that I have to check on security in the office and James needs to scan in some of his A Level work to support his predicted grades.

I'm saying that this is the story for any vigilant officer of the law who may challenge us on the half mile journey but in actual fact that is exactly what we are doing. We arrive at the office unchallenged by any armed forces and set about scanning in the essays. It takes a bit longer than we anticipated – wow, that boy does a lot of writing, bless him.

I get busy putting all the scanned work into documents with titles such as Meta Ethics – it all goes over my head, but I can cut and paste like a demon!

We get home in time for the breakfast slot and a quick go at the jigsaw before I brave a trip to Lidl to try to get more provisions. At the breakfast table I suddenly become quite tearful at the thought of going out. I don't feel fearful for my life, it's not a bloody zombie apocalypse, but I live in a permanent fear of doing the wrong things in social settings. Shaun has never let me forget about the time that he suggested we sat in better seats at the cinema and I worried on so much that we eventually moved to our ticketed seats.

Who knows what the rules are now? Am I going to fall foul of the new rules that people have settled into while

I've been staying at home, protecting the NHS and saving lives?

The chaps reassure me, and Shaun offers to go but despite his best efforts he can't really master the art of shopping for a week by planning meals. He's never lived down a recent shopping list of his which read "flour and something for tea". How would he cope when mid-shop you have to change the menu because key ingredients are missing?

So off I go with a warm coat at the ready in case I have to queue outside – some supermarkets have started a "one in, one out" policy with customers queuing outside, the requisite two metres apart.

Thankfully there is no need at Lidl and I go straight in.

All seems calm and reasonably stocked. It's amazing how quickly we've got used to seeing some empty shelves. Over the last decades we've come to expect everything to be available – no restrictions on seasonal fruit for example and we certainly expect things like flour, eggs, pasta to be there in volume… not today.

The other customers are quietly getting on with it and buying modest amounts, no stockpiling in evidence. By comparison, I look like I'm doing a panic buy. I need a badge that says "I have three hungry men at home" but perhaps that would look a bit wrong?!

I get home in one piece, wash my hands as advised by the people in the know and put the shopping away. We have enough food for another week so that's a relief.

We all get on with our work on various computers in the house which puts strain on the Wi-Fi. Once finished James and I take the dogs out for their night-time walk. We go through the wood, avoiding the dead rat I found earlier in the week. Apparently with all the restaurants closed the rats have abandoned the empty commercial bins and have started to come to the suburbs.

We go on to the golf course so the dogs can get a good run. When all this is over the golf course will be reclaimed by walkers which is only right. All that space for a daft game.

Spike finds a golf ball and proceeds to do his gymnastic routine. Honestly, he's like the little Olympians who have managed to make "the ribbon" an actual sport. He throws the ball in the air and flicks his front legs up, wiggles his head and his bum then gathers up the ball and runs a bit. Then, does it all again.

Arthur has no interest in the ball but can't see Spike having fun indefinitely so eventually pinches it and runs off. All for complete and utter badness.

We get home bang on time as Shaun has made a tea of salmon, new potatoes and veg. Also prawn cocktail to start. Very 1970's which is fab, and he even has retro music playing via Alexa.

Glass of wine, tea, great chat with the gang, all with a Disney plus film to watch… phew it's Friday.

Whippet Wordery - Spike

We got to go on the big dog play park today. It's awesome. It has stretches of grass for galloping, woods for exploring and little beaches.

I'm not good at digging but my brother is brilliant. He gets frustrated with me and shoves me out of the way to "show me how it's done". That's a bit annoying.

But the best bit is that there are little white balls dotted about. I blooming love them and I love throwing them up in the air. They're great.

Day 6: Saturday 28ᵗʰ March

Our esteemed leader, Johnson, has contracted the virus. In early March he was busy "reassuring the nation" by saying "oh, I've been into hospitals and been shaking hands with people, it's absolutely fine". Oh dear, it's a Government credibility disaster zone.

We'll keep on staying at home then.

We have a great day ahead. It's wine delivery day. And as if that is not enough, my new e-bike is also due to arrive. Both of these purchases don't go hand in hand except in a French village, so we'll give that a go.

I had promised the gang pancakes for breakfast so while Shaun does his approved one piece of exercise, walking the dogs (not sure how that will be policed actually – people sticking to one piece of exercise that is, not Shaun actually going out!), Archie and I set about making the pancake batter. Archie is the best at whisking all the lumps out and is also very good at eating the batter with a spoon but that's allowed today.

Shaun returns and gets the ham and cheese prepared for his pancakes but has a mild rebellion against my ration rule of half a slice of ham per pancake/per person. I realised yesterday that all the chaps are hungry because I'm giving them about double the portions that I tend to eat. It's not enough apparently and I fear they'll start fading away. You don't have to go mad though so for now Shaun goes against his natural greed and puts the packet of ham back before it's completely finished, with me exclaiming "there's another full meal in that you know". He looks unconvinced and I realise that I sounded just like my Nanny. I resolve to embrace more of my Scottish frugal roots!

One great consequence of all this "confined to barracks" stuff is that me and the boys, as self-confessed home birds are no longer running the risk of Shaun saying something like "ooh let's go to Belsay Hall/ Druidge Bay/Tynemouth Market". We know we are at home all weekend. Lovely.

So, the home entertainment is "pancake fest" followed by the clearing out the baking cupboard. Perhaps a trip to a National Trust property would have been preferable for the boys?

The audit of the baking supplies has an end game though. I've done a little itinerary of fun things to do every couple of days, akin to the day trips and activities on a holiday and Tuesday's "excursion" is afternoon tea!

Now, I'm not saying that I don't bake very often but quite a lot of the items in the cupboard are out of date. I have bread yeast, which is a mere three years past the sell by date and other items are four years. But the clear winner are the almonds with a date of seven years in the rear-view mirror of food safety. Quite a worry really as they start off with a long shelf life and we changed the kitchen five years ago so they must have been out of date then!!

Oh dear. Anyway, all tidy now and safe.

First delivery arrives, the case of wine, an essential for a lockdown and now securely in the house. And the lovely e-bike is due any moment. That's very exciting.

Archie and I get wrapped up because it's freezing outside and we set about sorting the garage ready for the new arrival. But no sooner had we stepped outside than Paddy from the bike shop arrived. With a lack of ceremonial pizazz, he quietly says "here's your new bike". It took me a little minute to take it in but yes here it is and it's brilliant.

Paddy puts the all-important lock on and shows me how all the electrics work. He demonstrates how easy it is to take the battery off – that did not look easy at all, compounded by me staying two metres away and not really being able to see anything he was doing. Ah well.

Paddy goes and leaves us with our new family member. I've never been one for giving inanimate objects names, but I might make an exception with my new bike. I'll have to give it some thought. Archie reckons maybe Van Gogh but wasn't he a renowned grumpy fellow? And I could do with a female companion in my life.

Me and the boys take it in turns to pedal round the block, judging the right time to switch it to the highest speed of Turbo. I think the boys just have it on the fast, whizzy setting all the time whereas I'm a bit old-school and "life has to be hard work" about the whole affair!

Once they've all had a play with my new mode of transport, I set off to go for my first bike ride.

I aim to use as little electrical support as possible (see martyrdom comment from earlier) and that is going really well until I hit the full force of the headwind at Balliol Park. It was like hitting a brick wall, so I crank it up to Turbo at that point, why not? The boys are right, it's fun!

I get back home 40 minutes later, having had a great time but learning that I need something to cover my ears and also warmer gloves. Brrrrr.

I warm up by doing a bit of journaling and having a glass of wine. What a nice day and a lovely way to spend an afternoon. I'm not put off by Shaun's grunts and puffs as he does his daily workout in the kitchen next to me. Sounds painful but the only bit that is definitely off putting is when he puts the resistance band around the table leg which, with every tug, slightly moves the table I am leaning on. My writing may have been affected in places, although it could similarly be the wine!

Day 7: Sunday 29ᵗʰ March

I wake up really early as I'm a bit achy. That'll be the arthritis for you… not the new bike, oh no, my new bike would never hurt me! But also, I would like a little bit of time by myself. Time by myself is hard to find at the best of times but now it's absolutely impossible. I'm a total out and out extravert but even I need a little bit of solitude in order to regroup my brain.

Shaun understands completely so I come downstairs to watch a bit of crappy TV and stumble across Father Brown on BBC iPlayer. Wait till the boys hear about this next step on my "road to being a boomer!"

I have a nice little watch and a therapeutic knit – I say therapeutic as it's relaxing but it's doubly therapeutic as it has a purpose. A campaign knitting purpose and I love a bit of a campaign! To bring you up to speed, literally, drivers routinely hurtle through our little part of Newcastle, completely ignoring the 20mph limit. So, me and a few neighbours have started knitting 20 signs and have fashioned them into scarves for the trees. It keeps us feeling that we're doing something anyway.

When the boys appear much later, we have a lovely brunch of sausages and poached eggs which I faff about making the chef way in clingfilm so that they boil into a perfect little shape. Very professional even though I say so myself.

There is also much rejoicing as I have finally allowed the black pudding to get on the menu (not for me as it's horrid stuff). We bought it last week at our friend Vincent's butcher shop, but I've been repeatedly saying "we can make a full meal out of that, not just be a bit on the side", ooh err missus! As a lifelong gym goer, weight trainer, Shaun would have a steak as a garnish to a chicken dinner – I fear the boys are following his lead (mental note to self, resurrect the much fated but slightly successful Tofu Tuesday, to act as the weekly compensatory action to the meat protein addiction).

The stressful item on the agenda today is that James wants a haircut.

We have four sets of clippers in the house, and each one appears to have a different thing wrong with it – how does that even happen?

I start with the small ones which I think are technically beard trimmers and James begins to take on quite a tufty look. This won't be good when I allow him to get to a mirror. Thank goodness I didn't set up the utility room like a little barbers with him in front of the mirror watching the patchy progress. As I try my best, Shaun is hastily trying to find and repair the other clippers, so when I'm eventually ready to move on to James' other side I am armed with the big industrial heavy ones. Oh dear it's all looking a bit uneven and haphazard, but James seems relaxed about it. I suppose we could always opt for a very close shave as a last resort.

I try a third set of clippers and in some goldilocks themed turn of events, they are just right.

Another fifteen minutes to get through all his layers of hair and we're done. What a change and this new short look is going to take a bit of getting used to. He goes to the mirror and laughs loudly while I'm still anxiously waiting for him to be annoyed. He sees my face and reassures me with "it's good Mum and let's face it I'm not going to see anyone!" I suppose that's true.

Lockdown haircut achieved and Shaun and I have a bottle of Prosecco between us to round off the week. James makes himself a Manhattan cocktail and it is fun to get the cocktail shaker out, so we'll have to do that again… another slippery slope identified.

Full week done on this lockdown business, what have we learned?

1. People can be a bit weird. Whether they're panic buying, walking in groups (not allowed), speeding through the village or jumping into the grass verge in case your dog touches them… they can be alarmingly strange.
2. Shaun and the boys eat a lot. I already knew that really, but wow, having to cater for them all is a full-time bloody job.
3. Alcohol is going to help.
4. It's amazing how little washing we have when we're not at work and school.

5. Work is overrated but still something I am anxious about.

6. The dogs are a tonic, although I secretly think they're getting a little bit tired of us being around all the time.

7. I need female company.

8. Zoom calls are easy, quite good fun and will definitely be used more in the future – down with unnecessary travel and up with the green agenda!

9. A lot of what we do is totally unnecessary. With large swathes of the population no longer driving to offices to spend time with people they don't like, doing tasks they don't care about in order to buy things they don't need, I wonder if we will rethink the whole madness.

Just before lockdown started, a friend remarked to me that a society is only ever 72 hours away from anarchy. Well, I'm not going to round this list up to a neat 10. That's the kind of unprecedented behaviour we're dealing with now. Anarchy!

Week 2

Day 8: Monday 30th March

I wake up really early which is odd because I went to bed irresponsibly late. I wasn't living the high life but was contentedly knitting, watching MasterChef and sipping red wine.

Time had slipped by happily and me and the dogs didn't go to bed until about one o'clock in the morning. So what the hooting hell am I doing waking up at 5:30am?!

Anyway, I finally get up about 6:45am as I definitely need to wash my hair today – I haven't bothered washing it since about Friday, maybe Thursday. No-one cares about that at the moment but it's now even annoying me, so it must be bad.

I decide to let the boys sleep for an extra hour because James wasn't feeling too well last night. He's got a breathless feeling, no fever and only a slight cough but in these paranoid times, it's a worry. I try not to panic but still check on him as he continues to sleep – when your little boy is 17 and six foot two, you still check.

We have our lockdown porridge together. Now that we don't have a jigsaw to do, you'd think we would finish quickly but we don't, we sit about having a chat and I have to dash to commute to work. Phew, I make it to the other side of the kitchen table for my 10am webinar with the CBI.

Today they're talking about which businesses must close and which ones can stay open. I thought it had been quite clear from the Government guidance but actually it's worth going over it again. There are whole swathes of industry who can't work from home and need to keep going, mainly manufacturing. It's still a "no" for Sports Direct so I hope the trainers do last out!

I then have my little daily Zoom call with my great colleague and even better friend Linda. It's nice to check in with her. I probably could get some of the Government money by classing her as furloughed, but I like knowing she is there, and it keeps us both going. In truth, I have a deep-seated fear that if I close the doors to the office, I will not re-open them. All those years of hard work snuffed out in a few short weeks.

For lunch today I'm going to attempt ratatouille. There are two reasons. Firstly, when Shaun went shopping one day last week, he bought two random courgettes. "What for?", I had enquired. No answer.

Secondly, we watched the Disney film of the same name recently so it's a laugh. Archie says that he hopes when he tastes it, like in the film, he will be transported back to his childhood... presumably in Disney rural France rather than his culinary disastrous upbringing in the North East of England.

I'm reminded of two low points in my maternal cooking career. The first one being when I was busy scrubbing a pan, in an attempt to get the burnt remnants of scrambled egg from the bottom. I shouted after a retreating Archie "when I went to the effort to make bloody scrambled eggs for breakfast, it would be really helpful if you actually ate them". To which the spikey four-year-old retorted "Mum it would be really helpful if you could actually make them". Ouch, but on reflection, fair enough.

The second embarrassment was a couple of years later involving the very stressful school parties. I didn't get to the list quick enough for the selection of what to contribute to one of the little afternoon teas. All the other sharper parents had selected the easy options of Quavers, grapes, bread sticks, raisins and the like. I was left with tuna sandwiches and had to ring Linda to find out how to make the tuna stick together inside the bread. Yes, you read that right. In my defence it was a long time ago. It's mayonnaise, in case you didn't know. You're welcome.

So today I have progressed to ratatouille. It turns out that it's not that hard to make and I bulk it out for the hungry chaps with a baked potato each. Later in the afternoon there is a request for toast (Shaun) which is denied by the café KGB. How much carbohydrates do you people actually need?

Day 9: Tuesday 31st March

I'm up early having slept well and right through – RESULT!

Off I go on the bike (no name yet) to the office to check on things, print off stuff and tidy up various financial items. It's the final day of the financial year. God knows how the accounts will look this time next year but let's not worry about that just now.

Back home for breakfast and no-one really fancies porridge this morning so it's a free for all of toast, Weetabix, juice and coffee. We still have time for a little chat before I cause shock and awe at the breakfast table by starting the process of breaking up the Disney jigsaw. Well I figure that we need the space for the afternoon tea and also we can do the jigsaw again in a couple of weeks... this lockdown business is going to run and run and by all accounts is going to be a marathon, not a sprint.

In the afternoon I set about doing the baking for the afternoon tea. Victoria sponge, banana loaf and scones – it's amazing how far you can get with just a little bit of self-raising flour. What on earth are the people doing who have stockpiled all that flour? It must be like the Great British Flipping Bake Off all over the damn country. Alternatively, the flour will all be in the bin by January next year.

James had noticed on our village Facebook page that someone was appealing for self-raising flour to make a birthday cake for their daughter. The boys suggest we pretend to have a birthday in order to procure some, but I say no. Might do next week though!

Anyway, I get the table set with all my lovely flowery granny crockery which has been built up over the years via charity shops. Nothing matches but on mass it looks pretty cute. I make the sandwiches. Smoked salmon, tuna and cucumber and finally for Shaun, the adventurous ham option. We have pork pies (yum) and gala pie which, if you have not had the dubious pleasure, is some sort of potted meat surrounding a boiled egg and encased in pastry (yeuch).

Archie whisks the cream for the scones and makes the tea. James gets the wine glasses out – yes, we're breaking the no alcohol rule and have decided to go mad at 4pm on a Tuesday!

I elect to crack open the last bottle of white wine from our trip to Italy in September last year and it was just the right thing with our feast. Memories of Umbrian afternoons and chatting and tucking into lovely food stuff.

After tea we don't want to leave the table, so we stay for a quick game of Trivial Pursuit with oldies versus teenagers as the teams.

There is a hilarious episode when the boys, try to simulate surfing in an attempt to work out what "goofy foot" means. Is it the right or the left foot at the back of a surfboard? As a team of two the boys had to answer democratically but in true brother style one says left (Archie) and one says right (James). They do a quick game of rock, paper, scissors to decide who on their team would get their own way. James won so they went with "right" as the answer.

Wrong!

Huge cries and recriminations ensue. Are team games so loud and boisterous in other houses I wonder! We carry on with a few sudden death rounds – this is after Shaun and I had won of course, ha ha. We are not competitive at all in this house, are we?

Day 10: Wednesday 1st April

Nothing special booked in for today so it's just us four plus the animals going through our new little routine.

I get up and decide to put on sports gear in an optimistic but yet fated pretence of doing exercise later.

I get everyone rallied for breakfast with Archie being the last one yet to appear, causing Shaun to hurriedly ask what we could do for an April Fool.

James suggests that we all go out, leaving Archie to find an empty house. I put a stop to that idea on account of it being irresponsible in the times of lockdown, plus Archie may not notice and we'd have to come back in with no fanfare at all!

Shaun opts for a hasty and pretty horrid proclamation that Johnson had died of the virus. Archie wasn't fooled at all and in his usual relaxed manner simply stated "no he hasn't otherwise I would have got a message." Eh? How come Archie has a direct line to the Cabinet? We don't ask. He's not really a morning person and doesn't like follow up questions, especially before breakfast.

At 10am I have my webinar check in with the CBI about finance and how businesses could access grants and interest free loans. Yet again, very useful for clients but not relevant to me.

Companies like mine now have a special name – we are being called the "stranded middle"! Nice eh? We're not small enough to get self-employed support and not big enough that things like the rate relief or individual Government interventions will apply.

Hell, us service bods don't even have a lobbying body to speak on our behalf. Watch this, the support will all be in pubs, restaurants, shops and aviation – who needs the service sector anyway?!

Nice to have a name though, even if it has the victim word of "stranded" in it!

The pressing issue for today is to get dog food. We're going to run out of the raw dog food in the freezer so Shaun does some ringing round to see if we can get an order. Going out to get pet supplies is classed as one of the approved reasons for a journey so we're fine.

He finds a pet food supplier in Hendon in Sunderland. It's not the most salubrious part of the North East but the dog food place turns out to be "canny and cheap", so worth the trip.

When James elects to go out for the drive, we have a chat about whether this was breaking the rules but we think they should be ok. He hasn't been out at all and we figure he could probably do with some sort of change of scene.

His report later includes the words "well dodgy" and the fact that they had kept a close eye on the car for fear of it being pinched for ram-raiding.

For those who don't know the term ram-raiding, it was started in the North East and is a form of breaking and entering which involves taking a vehicle and literally ramming it through a shop window and stealing all the stuff. I mention it because I noticed on the news that it's started up again... in Sunderland, how about that? Presumably this time it's not for TVs as it was in the 1990's but rather to pinch toilet rolls and self-raising flour.

Day 11: Thursday 2nd April

I woke up at 4am this morning and my mind was racing with all the things that I had to do, as well as worrying about all the things I couldn't control. At any time of the day both of those mind activities are pointless and at 4am they are annoyingly persistent.

Perhaps it was falling asleep while watching Question Time on my phone. The "discussion", also known as "sniping", was really unsettling.

There was a representative from the NHS trying to be heard. Hospitals and social care are having the toughest time. In fact, one of our dog walking friends who is an anaesthetist has told us that they have cancelled all planned surgeries including lifesaving cancer procedures. This means that she is having to ring people to tell them. She said the hospital where she works isn't under strain yet, but they are planning for it to be.

That's the reality. People are getting phone calls to say that they are not going to be treated but meanwhile on the screen, it's just arguments and political point scoring.

So, I went to sleep with a burning anger shrouded in a layer of dispiriting fatalism. That's what Greggs sausage rolls will be in hell! I amuse myself with that little thought in an attempt to calm my fretting and furious mind.

I finally get up at 7am and organise the porridge for everyone. I feel like I'm in a cowboy movie or maybe I am a farmer getting breakfast for everyone before they go out into the fields for the day. Yep, more little mind ramblings. Lockdown is clearly taking its toll as the daft stories are now constantly running in my head as I go about doing the same things each day.

We have a nice little breakfast at our allotted time according to the café opening hours which is just as well as I have three conference calls to do before 11:30am.

Lunch with the chaps was a "use up the salad" and cheese on toast affair but it seemed to go down well and the fridge is looking an organised empty. Good fridge and cupboard management is the key. I say that a lot when the chaps turn up their nose at any of my strange little meals, rustled up from things that are about to be "on the turn"!

The near empty fridge is at the point where we could justify a trip to Lidl tomorrow. Or shall I brave Asda where I can at least do self-scanning – is that a safer way to shop? Yes, that probably is the better idea and while I'm at it, I might also get a bottle of nice gin! That's that decided then. Safety and gin are the shopping considerations.

This afternoon our activity is a games session but at 4pm everyone is still working away on their various things. James is beavering away on his A Level portfolio, I'm investigating how to do training sessions on Zoom (our COVID survival plan) and Shaun is writing a blog. Archie is having a bit of a break, playing on his phone after finishing his work and doing his daily exercise outside which involved an exhausting routine of press ups, squats and sit ups – his version of PE.

We eventually come together at about 4:30pm for a few rounds of games starting with the most ridiculous thing that Linda had bought us for Christmas. It's really hard to do it justice in a literary description but here goes.

The "player" has to put on a headpiece (bear with me) and calibrate it to their heartbeat... mmmm? Then the rest of the players throw the dice and act out what the dice says in order to wind up the "head gear guy". Types of wind up activities included "acting like a zombie", "shouting" or inexplicably "making pig noises".

Staying calm and therefore in the "green zone" means you get one point but if you get wound up and go into the red, you get no points.

The summation of the results is that James is easy to wind up, getting into fits of giggles at the drop of a hat, or in this case at people pretending to be zombies. Shaun is pretty neutral. Archie is the chillaxed clear winner. And I get wound up when I think their high jinks are going to spill my cup of tea.

That is a good illustration of our respective personalities. Who needs any profiling other than that? I might start using the game at work!

Day 12: Friday 3ʳᵈ April

12 – now that is a significant number for two reasons. Firstly, early on in this shitstorm, 12 days was promoted as the lockdown or quarantine period.

So yay, it's over... nope. Secondly, we are now starting to get our heads round the fact that actually this is a 12 weeks thing, minimum.

At work I often refer to the well understood Kubler-Ross transition curve and now we are probably in the bargaining phase where we are thinking that we might need to adapt, to do things differently.

I amuse myself doing the COVID-19 version which includes a "gin peak" early on, as well as a middle section of small peaks and bigger troughs simply captioned "Eh?" followed by "WTF". The more determined move into the next upward curve section on my drawing has the word "Right!" as a label. Everyone knows that if you say "Right!" in a firm and clear way, it means you are "on it".

The morning routine is now… a routine, so maybe we are moving along the curve.

Quick trip to the office on the bike and home for breakfast with the gang. It's amazing how quickly you get into a new groove. I'm aware that my biking habit is still in the "enthusiastic beginner" phase and that this little bit of new joy will fade over time but for now, once I'm finished my work, I come home the long way round just for fun.

We have a lovely family breakfast and a little chit chat about the day ahead before I have to finally steal myself and go to the supermarket.

Despite yesterday's gin-influenced decision, I'm still undecided about the choice of supermarket. These are the big decisions now. Encouraged by the boys, I put my dilemma into the virtual hands of the decision wheel app on my phone. I enter Asda; Sainsburys; Aldi; Lidl; Don't bother.

The "don't bother" option causes a bit of concern amongst the troops, but I only did it to play with the notion of staying at home and not running the gauntlet. I'm sure I could rustle something up from the depths of the freezer.

It comes up as Sainsburys, but I realise that there is less risk if I go to Asda as I can do self-scanning and I know where everything is. How very odd to think about minimising health risks on a trip to get messages (for non-Scottish readers that's groceries).

It's also odd to get in the car and actually drive as I've all but stopped using it. The car needs to go in for a repair and they're going to pick it up next week. I don't know when I'll get it back especially as they have to quarantine it for 72 hours before they even start the work. But I've elected not to bother getting a hire car. That would have been unheard of just a few weeks ago. Maybe we can keep some new habits permanently?

I get to Asda and it seems quiet. Is it closed? No, but the security people are only letting a few people in at a time and therefore customers are forming a queue outside with trolleys while staying the required two metres apart.

I get a trolley and take my place at the back. At first it doesn't seem very long, but I quickly realise that it snakes around the roped area in the same way that they do at Disney. The difference being this rollercoaster is the dodging of an invisible virus that may just kill me while I'm trying to get food for my family. That sounds melodramatic but just today the news broke that two perfectly healthy (no underlying health issues) female nurses had died of this damn thing. If that doesn't put the frighteners up you to make you stick to the rules, what will?

I get as much on the list as I can, and the shopping experience isn't too bad. Still no flour and no pasta. The queuing and the empty shelves are a bit reminiscent of my trips to Russia in the late 1990's except the Great British Public aren't quite as good at sticking to the rules, taking orders from people in uniform or doing it all in silence.

Although at times Asda is eerily quiet and everyone looks a little bit depressed, so it is a bit like the Moscow underground. There are still couples out shopping together and staff are chit chatting away to each other as normal, which feels just a bit weird.

I get home and put the shopping away – that's us stocked up for another few days, maybe a week if we're careful. There's no other option as the delivery slots are booked up for weeks and people who are in the vulnerable category and shielding should get priority anyway.

I give my hands a thorough scrub which is still the main advice.

"Wash your hands". It's still alarming to realise that large swathes of the population have to be told to do this basic act of personal hygiene. In fact, on Twitter early into this whole crisis a guy had tweeted that he'd noticed for the first time there were queues for the sinks in the gents. They haven't taken any sinks out you know! Shudder.

Day 12: Friday 3rd April

This is new! Starting a new little book part way through a day, but it has to be done for two reasons.

Firstly, I used up the remainder of the current journal by capturing all the detail of the first part of my day, the surreal trip to Asda. In the future people may not believe it or even imagine it happened. We take so much for granted that a few weeks ago it would have been impossible to envision empty shelves, security guards, queuing to get in and a one-way system to control the small number of customers.

Secondly, I don't want to skimp covering the event of the week and that is James getting to the A-Level finishing post.

The A-Level exams have been cancelled and that didn't even happen during the Second World War! What James needed to do was to send in previously marked work to help the teachers to back up their predicted grade and assessment of his work.

The marks are still uncertain of course and the added worry for one of James' teachers is that she is a self-confessed hard task master. That's good in the normal course of events but this year she marked the mocks in her usual "final kick" manner and now she has to justify what "they should have won".

As a result, James has been working really hard over the past couple of weeks, making sure he had all his previous work in good order and scanned in. This endeavour has culminated in his teacher phoning and telling us that James has done brilliantly. He's apparently "responded with intelligence", "has been a complete joy" and has made "the teachers' job easy". She can't say for certain, but she is as reassuring as she can be.

She ends the call with some additional work: "James, I have one final piece of work for you and it's this. Ask Mum or Dad to give you an education in whisky or beer and work hard at it over the weekend. Oh, and also watch films."

And this from the teacher who has been the one who has mostly said to the boys to work hard, behave, shower more often, work hard, don't drink, work hard, grow up, listen, work hard... you get the picture.

She is so complimentary, I could actually burst with pride! Well done James.

Day 13: Saturday 4ᵗʰ April

Shaun wakes up thinking that there's someone at the door, so he gets up and dashes downstairs. He's always like that, dashing to the door, leaping to his phone when it rings. I just take my time and if I miss people then so be it. Anyone who knows me knows that my phone is on permanent silent and I never answer it. Dispelling the stereotypes of introvert and extrovert right here in this paragraph!

I manage to stay half asleep throughout the whole charade until such time as he must have decided it was getting up time anyway and shouts upstairs "do you want a cup of coffee sweetheart?"

I try to stay asleep.

"SWEETHEART, do you want a cup of coffee? A COFFEE, SWEETHEART?"

I screw my eyes shut.

"A COFFEE, SWEETHEART?"

I eventually answer, "go on then".

It's sodding ten to sodding seven and I was actually asleep!

Shaun brings up said coffee which is a nice thing to do but it's still before seven in the sodding morning. Have I said that? On a Saturday, I haven't said that!

We watch an episode of Vera which, if you're from the North East, is doubly brilliant as you get to play the Vera game, which goes something like this:

Shout "ooh that's Spanish City/the RVI/the Vermont Hotel" or any other landmark.

Shout "wow she got from Teeside to Rothbury in double quick time there, mind", "in a Land Rover"!

Shout "why is she going over the Tyne Bridge, that's a stupid way to go".

Shout "oh look there's Sean Kenney/Karen Traynor/Philip Harrison" or any other North East actor friends of ours.

Say (no need to shout this one as it's not exciting) "that's the part I'd get" levelled at actors who say nothing and do something unglamorous like digging a hole, opening a door or falling silently off a building.

Shout (back to shouting) "oh it can't be him/her, too obvious" because anyone who has watched the programme knows, the guilty party is ALWAYS the least obvious person.

Sigh (ooh new one) "why does she always go to a skanky part of the region, honestly she hardly shows us in the best light", as if Brenda Blethyn personally chooses the locations.

This episode doesn't disappoint on the "unlikely guilty party" front because it turns out to be the pregnant girlfriend of one of the main suspects who was no longer a suspect on account of him dying in a petrol bomb accident... are you keeping up?

Vera solved for the day and Shaun takes the dogs out while I move from watching the TV in bed to watching the TV from the sofa. Very strenuous that and a complete re-enactment of the joke picture doing the rounds on social media at the moment with a woman in bed saying "I must get up, I'm late for the sofa."

It's film fest day in the activity calendar after all so I'm only securing my seat early!

It's Shaun's turn for the film first but the old one he wanted can't be found. While he is thinking again, I elect for the Hitchcock classic The Lady Vanishes. The film doesn't disappoint as it has lots of stars, great characters and just enough intrigue to keep us going. With the old brilliant films, you can also spot the little devices and plot lines that have appeared in other films over the years, well according to the film buffs in the room. All slightly lost on me as I get carried away by the obvious storyline.

James also points out later that for an old film it manages not to be sexist thus negating the need for me to exclaim "hashtag me too" at regular intervals in an attempt at ensuring the boys don't see the plot/characterisation as normal in any way. We often like a classic James Bond but dear me, I'm busy during those films!

We completely fail in our attempt at a four-film day, only managing to top off our viewing with one more, the excellent choice from Archie of Toy Story 2.

It's a double header day today with Indian Take Away also on the itinerary. I put in the order while the boys have a quick cricket bowl outside. I am just about to complete the order when I succumb to the cries of "oh we need more chips this time" and "can I have a starter". As I finally press "confirm" on my phone, I realise there is enough food on order to feed an army, so that must be about right for this lot.

About an hour later, the same driver as last week appears at the door with the takeaway and starts with the embarrassing instruction of "just like last week, I'll leave it here on the drive and you can get it". I appreciate his compliance with the new COVID rules but typically at the moment of "just like last week" about a hundred of our neighbours walk by. Thank goodness I hadn't compounded my slovenly image by being in my pyjamas.

We scoff our lovely treat of takeaway (now a weekly occurrence as the entire area knows) and as predicted by self, there is a whole bag of chips left.

Apparently, I am absolutely NOT TO THROW ANYTHING AWAY – Shaun still tells the story of me throwing away left over takeaway early on in our relationship. He said it was nearly a deal breaker!

Day 14: Sunday 5th April

Day 14 of trusting the Great British Public to self-isolate. It's forecast to be lovely weather, so everyone is gearing themselves up for people deciding that "the beaches will be deserted, so let's go".

The message could not be clearer... stay at flipping home! And if you all have that thought, the beaches will not be deserted now will they?

What shall we do today? There's nothing big in the calendar. No film fest, no takeaway, no afternoon tea. Ah well, we'll just have to hang out together and have a nice Sunday.

Shaun and I both take the dogs for their morning walk. This is allowed as we're both from the same household but it does mean that we've both had our one bit of approved exercise for the day so the boys will have to do the afternoon/evening walk in case we get spotted and reported to the KGB. Like old Russia again, maybe people will start to "dob in" their neighbours.

We are met by the dogs' whippet girlfriend, Lucy, on the golf course and the pack of hounds have a great run around while us humans stay over two metres apart for a little chat. That's not really allowed I'm sure but it's lovely to chat to Carol even though her judgement of two metres seems to ebb at times. I resolve to bring a stick the next time. That sounds bad!

We get back home, and Archie is up, so I ask him for his breakfast order. He elects for porridge which is a surprise as it's the weekend so he could have gone for bacon and eggs. It's this lack of flour business that has foxed him I reckon because the absolute first choice for a weekend brunch would normally be pancakes.

I get a text from the boys' Dad, to enquire about them going to him for a spell. This sends me into a mild panic as I just don't want to let them out of my sight.

What if they get ill, what if I get ill, what if we as a country go into full lockdown and I can't get them back, ever... the mild panic has the potential to spiral.

He had suggested that the boys go to his house tomorrow but putting my anxiety to one side we could all probably do with a couple of days to get prepared, so I suggest Wednesday. That means we can watch the news just in case the Government elects to clamp down after people spend the sunny Sunday flouting the rules and gallivanting around the parks and beaches.

For now, though, let's enjoy the day. We have our breakfast outside, complete with the whippets wandering around exploring the garden, also known as trampling on the new plant shoots coming through.

After breakfast the boys decide to do a press up competition. James nips upstairs to put on socks (crucial apparently) and comes back down with a report of a leg strain/injury. You can imagine the ribbing he got for that from his competitive and sarcastic younger brother? Despite his "injury" the competition goes ahead.

I'm counting James' effort and Shaun is assigned to Archie detail.

Off they go! Pretty impressive by both boys but Archie wins with a count of 31. All his training is definitely paying off. Maybe by the end of this lockdown we'll be in great shape. Ha ha, given that I've been eating three meals a day like the chaps, and sporadically doing the odd bit of yoga, I doubt I'm going to be in the shape of my life! I mention this and all James says is "round is a shape". Harsh but true.

The boys start hovering about the kitchen looking hungry, so I offer to make the traditional lunchtime dish from Madrid – egg and chips! I kid you not. When I went to Madrid to visit friends, they did a great job of showing off the culture and part of it was the signature city dish of egg and chips. To be fair it was well seasoned potato wedges with perfectly cooked egg drizzled over the top which looked amazing. I couldn't eat it at the time as runny egg is a no-go when pregnant. Wow, that was over 18 years ago I realise as I try to recreate it for my six foot two little baby.

My key ingredient is the left-over bag of chips. This brings about the inevitable cry of "told you that extra bag was needed"! I fear that the "extra bag" will be a new "tradition". The boys have an opportunistic habit of locking these in, secure in the knowledge that I love a

wee tradition or two. I'm being managed very well by
the hungry gang or I'm being "owned" as they would
say. I don't mind though.

Whippet Wordery - Spike

*That cat says he's going to kill me. To be
honest, he says it most days and then sends
me "warnings" by hiding behind the kitchen island
and jumping out. It fair gives me a fright.*

*But the great thing now is that The Family are at home
all the time. It's brilliant.*

*The cat gets a row for his angry antics and if I get stuck
on my way upstairs by him meanly standing half way
up blocking my path, someone finds me and gives me a
guide past. The cat's furious.*

*The cat says his time will come. I don't know what that
means but he seems really pleased with himself.*

Whippet Wordery - Arthur

*The cat's an idiot. I give him a good chase sometimes
and he hides under human Mum's bed.*

*He stuck a claw in my face once and human Dad went
totally ballistic. Something about me losing an eye but
that'll never happen. I'm too quick.*

*The Family are at home all the time now, so I don't get
a good chase in.*

*The cat says the chasing never bothered him anyway.
He's lying. He's an idiot.*

Week 3

Day 15: Monday 6th April

Well, we are now one day overdrawn on the original "stay at home for a couple of weeks" storyline.

I wake up feeling that I haven't slept and am also now fretting that the boys are off to their Dad's in a couple of days.

I reckon we may all have lost a bit of confidence in letting our loved ones out of our sight. They could fall ill, there may be a full lockdown! It's like a combination of two historical events potentially happening in my head simultaneously – the plague and the building of the Berlin wall.

This, at 3am in the morning is a very worrying and distressing train of thought.

My friend Clare posts on Facebook, *any of my friends keep wakening up at 3am?*

I respond with, *Yes, what the hell is all that about?*

Apparently, Clare replies, *Dawn French was on the radio with a theory that those anxiety moments are to remind us of the things that happened thirty years ago?*

I'm not sure about that as I can't remember anything in my past resembling this freaking scenario.

Anyhoo, I'm up. It's Monday morning and I'm totally exhausted. I decide that if the boys are going to their Dad's imminently, then two things need to happen. Firstly, I'm going to take the day off work and that sodding VAT return can sodding well wait till later in the sodding month!

Secondly, the boys can have a bit of a lie in and we can have a treat breakfast as it is the start of their Easter holidays after all, not that we've really noticed that happening.

We do have a nice breakfast and as it turns out it's the usual "during the week porridge" but with the full production of fruit and honey and maple syrup as accompaniments!

The main job today is to get all the bike tyres pumped up. I have my new bike of course, ha ha, check me. Shaun has a chunky green "manly" bike which is old and only keeps going with the help of WD40 – everyone knows that WD40 is a magic substance. And the final one in the trio is my ancient one lurking in the garage, unloved. I work out that it must be about thirty years old – maybe that's what I'm worrying about?

It's not the good side of ancient, you know in the way of say a classic French looking jalopy, with a cute basket on the front. No this is a 1980's red and yellow "style over substance" hybrid, which is too heavy, too slow and quite frankly hard work – in a way that makes you wish you'd walked!

With tyres all pumped up, me and the two boys set off down the bridlepath on a test ride. There are even more people out walking who have never walked in their lives, or at least not since 1979. It's funny isn't it that when you restrict something, people make sure they "get their share". Maybe we should keep it going somehow! It could help the health of the nation.

It's hard to dodge them though, but we manage. Then we go to the cycle path next to the business park. Do these new cycle lanes give you right of way when they continue next to the zebra crossing? I just don't know so I end up hesitating at the crossing while the bus driver, who clearly knows the rules also stops and slowly but surely shakes his head. I can see the look. Yet another cyclist finding the bikes and setting off with no idea. I try to look confident and slightly haughty as I get my brood across the road without incident.

Stay at home; protect the NHS; save lives, I mutter guiltily to myself.

We have a nice little cycle for exercise but the advice/ edict from the Government is to only take your exercise about ten minutes from your home so at that mark I suggest we turn around.

We head back into a pretty strong headwind which encourages me to put the electric assist up a notch, not to the full Turbo as was the accusation later from the now puffing teenagers behind me!

We stop just before the zebra crossing, scene of bus incident earlier and Archie declares that he is knackered but also that his "bollocks are getting squashed". Nice! We agree we all liked the jaunt out though and plan to do it again tomorrow – if there is no lasting damage to the precious cargo! Maybe he'll wake up worrying about them in thirty years time?!

Day 16: Tuesday 7ᵗʰ April

I had a blissfully ignorant day yesterday away from my emails, my phone and updates on the TV. So, this morning I get up early to get back up to speed. I start with the news that the health of the Prime Minister has deteriorated to the extent that he is now in intensive care in hospital.

You would think that would be a bit of a wakeup call for people, but folks are still congregating, and Aston Villa Football Club has been spotted running a team training session in a public park. Oh dear.

There's going to be some backlash coming out of all of this and you'd wonder at the wisdom of high-profile enterprises so blatantly breaking the rules. They were bound to be spotted.

I also hear on the news that Ronaldo has given over his hotel to the NHS. Temporarily I am sure, but he's doing something. That'll not be the headline though will it, we all know that bad news and mudslinging sells more papers.

I get on with my emails until the chaps make an appearance, and I score lots of Mum points by making a brunch of bacon, eggs and avocado. Pretty nice and the eggs are done to perfection – I'm getting to be a dab hand at the technique of shrouding the eggs in clingfilm before boiling so that they come out a perfect shape. Very professional but the practice will have to stop when the clingfilm runs out. Since buying it (probably in the 1990's) I've become much more environmentally aware so won't be buying any more.

It's also a bit of a faff, which clarifies it in my mind that I wouldn't even get through the first round of MasterChef, as I have a very low faffing threshold.

I stop work for another day so I can make the most of the time with the boys. Off we go on the bikes again. Me on my new whizzy machine, Archie on Shaun's old rough terrain thingy and James bringing up the rear on my old rubbish bike.

Today we're off to the cricket club to check on security – my action from an email exchange about the place. Not for the first time, I remind myself that I am on too many committees!

I decide that crossing the Great North Road is probably too treacherous (even the spelling of that word is filled with doubt and anxiety!). We head up the usual bridlepath and therefore run the gauntlet of potentially COVID-19 riddled families who have just taken up walking and don't know there's a crisis on.

Unlike us who are going on a necessary journey, using a safe mode of transport and one at a time. Oh dear, wrong on all fronts there!

Stay in, stay safe, save the NHS, save lives.

We get to the Great North Road and I explain to the boys that there is a cycle path but it runs out and the road is really busy so we should maybe stop at the big roundabout and walk across the road using the pelican crossing. I explain it twice.

Archie says he still doesn't understand.

James tries to help by summing up with "just follow Mum and do what she does." I'm not sure that's the best advice so as I cycle off, I add a bit of my wisdom along the lines of "just remember that a lot of car drivers are complete tossers".

I just finish the sentence when a lycra clad skinny middle-aged man on a racing bike speeds past millimetres from my front wheel. I am therefore able to redress the balance by adding a timely "and so are a lot of cyclists to be fair".

We get to the roundabout and as it turns out there aren't many cars so we are able to scoot right over and execute the second stage of the plan which is to get to the cricket ground. This is turning out to be a stressful little journey. I can feel my paranoia building with the fear that we will have an accident which will be bad enough but also, we will be vilified for putting the NHS under pressure.

We get across the road safe and sound and I check the sports club shutters and post-box. I show the boys the stash of toilet roll and hand-wash in the storeroom – I know where to come when the going gets tough with supplies. The boys try to persuade me to unlock the upstairs bar and raid the beer and chocolate, but I explain that I would likely set off the alarm and we were supposed to be checking security, not breaching it. On reflection I should have been firmer on the moral reasons for not going on a thieving spree.

We set off again and after toodling along the first leg of the journey and getting to the roundabout I look behind. No fellow cyclists.

Oh good Lord, I think, Archie has come off, or there's a problem with one of the bikes. I make my way back up the road to be met by just Archie. Apparently, James had come off, so we wait. After a few minutes, in his usual style of calm underplaying of the situation, Archie says "oh I think he may have a problem with the bike and is waiting for you."

Problem with the bike! It's completely and utterly knackered but that's not my concern. Is James ok? What happened? Did a car hit him? Has he banged his head? What could have happened... oh my good god.

Turns out he hit a rut in the road then hit the kerb, then went flying over the handlebars onto the pavement. A car driver had stopped to check if he was ok, which he is, thank god... have I said that?

I give Shaun a ring to come on a mercy mission to pick up James and the knackered bike. When he arrives, he was as shocked as I was at the sorry sight, his early smile turning into a frightened looking face and lots of the same questions I had asked earlier.

We manhandle the broken bike into the mini – easier said than done. James apologises again. Bless him he's very sad about the whole thing and is feeling wretched. I'm just so relieved that he's ok and I couldn't give a damn about the bike.

I reassure him again that it's all ok and when we get home we have a glass of wine together – thank goodness we have the new Gosforth Fam Café rule of wine being allowed on a Tuesday.

STAY AT HOME. SAVE THE NHS, SAVE LIVES!

Day 17: Wednesday 8th April

Nationally the health crisis is getting worse. The "peak" that they talk about hasn't happened yet, and the daily death toll is continuing to climb. It's now up to over 900 which is desperately sad and hard to get your head round.

I can only focus on my world for now. The boys are going off to their Dad's today so my aim is to have a nice morning and make sure they get packed up and don't forget anything.

We can't just scoot up and down the road on a whim, there is a threat that the police will stop you and demand to know if you're journey is absolutely essential. I don't think the cry of "I wanted my football shorts" would cut the mustard! And perhaps "I got a computer part delivered to my Mum's by mistake" would be equally non bona fide!

As the boys get organised I do the final porridge for breakfast. I get a row from Shaun for calling it the final breakfast, but it is a little bit helpful to say it out loud.

I do a short stint of work and then join the boys outside in the garden for a quick game of cards. It is Shaun's game which is, according to James, a bit like gin rummy but it doesn't have a name that we know of.

As it turns out I come joint first with Shaun on a score of 103 which is poor show given that I started with two Jacks and they are the highest scoring cards in the game and should have set me up for a certain win... apparently! In reality I have absolutely no idea what is going on.

Our second game is curtailed as the people who "bagsied" the knackered bike from my Facebook post are due to call round in a few minutes. We all toodle off to the garage to get the wreckage out on the pavement and this instigates an impromptu clear out. You should always take the chance of lobbing stuff out.

Archie asks if he can go out on Shaun's electric scooter, which is lurking at the back, but I say that I doubt it has any charge in the battery. Archie, who is a crack negotiator asks, "if it has charge, can I go on it?"

Before I know it I've agreed and the damn thing does have sodding charge so off he goes... with me shouting after him "be careful, save the NHS!"

James gets his old kids bike out which is far too small for him but undeterred he sets off for races with Archie to the sounds of me screeching "no races, protect the NHS, save lives". I fear we've descended into a bike addicted family of renegades.

The boys' Dad arrives to pick them up, all too soon. I don't want them to go and judging by the number of final hugs I get from them, they can sense it.

And they're gone.

I have a little cry.

You'd think after being divorced for ten years I'd be used to the separation, but these are "unprecedented" times and very much a worry.

What to do now? I could catch up with work or could do a study session on my new certificate MOOC course from the University of Amsterdam in designing a cycling city (I'm an annoyingly evangelical new cyclist, like an ex-smoker!). But I can't be bothered and also, I have a book club meeting later and I haven't finished the book.

So, I lie in the garden and read the book. Lovely. And I don't feel guilty one bit, this lockdown has lots of advantages.

After preparing three meals a day for weeks I can't be bothered cooking or really eating so I have some yoghurt and Shaun fends for himself. Of course, he is perfectly capable and I reckon for the next ten days he might just need to take the lead role in the kitchen. Why not? I'm off duty! Although I'll probably interfere at some point, can't help myself.

Day 18: Thursday 9th April

I have my daily Zoom call with Linda and today I have to discuss the issue of her going on furlough. It's the financially sensible thing to do as I need to tap into support and hand on heart there isn't any work for her to do. But it still feels like the end of an era, the closing of a door that may not get re-opened again.

This was the main reason I hadn't done it till now but the timing is right, and I hope it allows Linda to do other things with her day without feeling she needs to constantly check her emails. She shouldn't feel that she needs to be available all the time.

Linda is, as always, the complete voice of reason, but we know that the next few weeks are going to be strange and probably tougher again. I've been awake since the "worry witching hour" of 3am fretting about it and my anxiety levels are still high. But they are overtaken by a sense of sadness and loneliness. My third child, my business, isn't on a life support machine but it has been evacuated to the country. If it survives, it won't forgive me.

I draft up what I hope is a reassuring letter for Linda. The way the process works is that she will be furloughed for a minimum of three weeks, but I don't need to (and can't anyway) stipulate a return date. My best guestimate at this stage is the 1st June but we'll just need to wait and see.

It feels awful though and after my call, I try to start up a conversation about it with Shaun. But he's embroiled in his frustration with video editing so, I take some time out, make a cup of tea, go into the cosy TV room and have a small cry.

I finish my last meeting at 7pm and I walk the dogs, have tea and spend a wee bit of time with a now grumpy Shaun. I'm assuming the video production hasn't gone well but I strategically don't ask!!

At 8pm we hear people out in the street clapping and banging pots, one firework goes off which in turn sets the dogs off a bit. Such is the Thursday tradition of coming out into the street to clap and show our appreciation and gratitude for the workers in the NHS.

It seems more poignant this week, with those two young nurses having died from the damn virus. They were two young mothers which is so tragic and they frighteningly had no underlying health issues, which is the expression we keep using secretly in our heads to convince ourselves that we would be fine.

The tragic deaths of these two young people brings into sharp relief the constant cry for better PPE for the frontline staff. They are putting themselves at great risk with every shift that they work.

And it's not just the medical staff of course. I was talking to my accountant earlier in the day and he said that one of his neighbours is a cleaner in a local hospital and she has no PPE at all. Nothing. On top of that she is under extreme stress as people are dying alone in the hospital, sometimes on trolleys and she even said this week that she was cleaning a toilet and found someone had died in a cubicle.

It's horrendous to think that this is the situation for the final moments for people. There's going to be a lot of emotional damage after the immediate health crisis.

But for now, we're on our doorstep clapping our little hearts out and hoping that we will be ok and that we are doing enough. For a moment in the street seeing the faces of my neighbours, making eye contact and with a watery smile mouthing "are you ok" across the noise, it feels really special.

For the second time today, I cry.

Day 19: Friday 10th April

It's Good Friday. Not that you'd notice a bank holiday in all this weirdness! Good Grief Friday more like.

We get out and about on the golf course with the dogs and have a happy time with Spike doing his "dance with golf ball" routine and Shaun trying to whip up interest in Arthur to chase a stick.

Then I spot it. A small deer standing right in the middle of the fairway staring at us and trying to work out in its tiny little brain when the right time would be to do a runner.

I grab Spike's collar and Shaun goes towards Arthur, but the timing is awkward. Arthur is now in full play mode so grabs the aforementioned stick, runs a short way off before spotting his new toy, abandoning the stick and legging it after Bambi.

He chases it from one side of the golf course to the other and back again in a slight comedy fashion reminiscent of scenes from Scooby Doo. Spike meanwhile is doing his dinger, straining at the collar to join his brother for the high jinks.

It's less funny when the deer jumps out of the golf course and onto the path with Arthur still hot on its heels. I can just imagine the walkers being faced with that scene and immediately doing some panic call to the police to say someone is out hunting animals.

We wait on the golf course for a bit as there's no real point going after him. Sure enough he returns and comes sauntering up to us absolutely exhausted. I make him come right up to me and tell him to sit down so he can receive his telling off, complete with finger pointing. But he lies down still panting and covered in little scrapes and unexplained green stains.

We set off for home with an exhausted Arthur and an annoyed Spike. Spike tries to assert his dominance by dog humping his brother – what's that all about?! I am often to be heard shouting some sort of instruction to the various house occupants and one of those is "stop humping your brother"! Just as well the neighbours are dog people and will know what's going on – I hope so anyway.

What an eventful little walk.

After a day in the garden, we have our tea of salmon and open a bottle of Prosecco because we have a Zoom call with our friends in Scotland, Mel and Kay. They are the inventors of Fizzy Friday so we might as well keep that going.

Leading up to the time of the Zoom call, Shaun does his usual thing when I've "encouraged" him to have a social commitment and it's this:

Me: We're calling Mel and Kay tonight.

Shaun: What? When?

Me: 7pm

Later

Me: Remember we're calling Mel and Kay.

Shaun: Are we? How?

Me: On Zoom.

Shaun: Oh

Later

Me: I'll just get the laptop.

Shaun: What for?

Me: So, we can call Mel and Kay.

Shaun: What? Now?

Later, by seconds

Me: How long has your TV programme got to go?

Shaun: Don't know, why?

Groan…

However, on the call we have a lovely load of chatter. By the end of the call Shaun is suggesting we extend our regular little weekends to Edinburgh and the like by going further afield such as Florence.

He's a reluctant socialiser but once he gets warmed up, he's hard to stop.

I fear that the lead up to this holiday idea will be a chore for his social secretary. I have this commitment recorded here though so can show him if he starts his shenanigans.

Day 20: Saturday 11ᵗʰ April

The death toll in the UK is set to hit 10,000 today.

It's a tragedy and really scary. The Prime Minister is apparently doing well so at least we won't have to deal with the Government descending into an internal turmoil. Unless they are already, how would we tell?

We haven't got much planned today but the weather is lovely so we might as well make the most of it!

A neighbour is giving away broccoli and cabbage seedlings so we're going to give them a go in the garden. All the Garden Centres are still closed and maybe cabbages will prove to be nicer than geraniums in any case.

On the way up to collect the seedlings we notice at one house there are three teenage girls just standing in the drive. Looks a bit odd until we realise that they're visiting granny who is standing in the doorway two metres apart from them. What a shame that grannies won't be getting hugs or even touched at all.

It's something we take for granted and it will be a miss for people. I'm lucky as I'm not a naturally huggy person but even I've noticed the contact quota reducing over this time.

Seedlings planted along with some out-of-date seeds that I found in the back of the shed, we feel we've done our bit for the garden. Who knows what will survive and as the seeds had a use by date of 2011, I'm not holding out much hope. I figure I might as well give them a go as they're not going to grow in the packet in the shed now, are they? Years ago, I had an allotment and my plot neighbour was a lovely old guy called Jack. He would say two things regularly. Firstly, "I'm eighty four you know" and secondly "Stick it in the groond Audrey, it'll live or die." So I've stuck stuff in the groond.

Later we had planned to go out on the dog walk together (very naughty as Shaun had already been out for his exercise earlier) but we realise one of us will have to stay in to receive the dog food order. We had piggy backed on next door's delivery at a time when the only piggy backing you are allowed to do is for deliveries. In fact, I'm assuming it's positively encouraged.

We have also ordered the now "traditional" Saturday night take away, so I elect to stay at home and deal with the arrivals.

Another consequence of COVID-19 is that people are suspicious of cash. I, for some time now, have had a love/hate relationship with good old-fashioned hard cash. I love it because you know where you stand and everyone who knows me knows I'm always "wedged up". I like about £80 in my purse at all times as that's the amount for:

1. A shop to feed the family for a bit,
2. A meal for two in case you have to stand the bill on your own for some reason, either due to necessity or for social reasons,
3. A hotel room.

As I write the list they come to my mind in reverse order. Make of that what you will!

Anyhoo, it's important to be wedged up, have some readies at your disposal. But I digress. The "hate" side of cash is that loads of people touch it… yeuch!

So now I'm faced with the Thai food delivery man leaving the thermos bag on the step saying "take the food out and put the 'enveloped' cash into the bag". Their debit card machine wasn't working when I rang. Apparently.

He asks if I need change and of course I say no. Then I realise that this doesn't leave much of a tip. But I fret that if I offer now, I'm going to look like a real cheapskate as I'd have to ask for change. I can't give a £20 tip would be a bit outlandish. Also, and more importantly it might be considered germ warfare if I start scrabbling around for the emergency fiver (I know I have one somewhere).

Socially awkward moment ensues so I say thank you again and "have a good night" and thank you again. Oh, good Lord, with coughing in someone's direction now being tantamount to GBH, maybe fluffing up your tip leaving etiquette is going to be some form of harassment.

Shaun compounds the now escalating social mess by arriving home at the same time. Thinking the delivery was the dog food, he makes idle chit chat by saying, "Oh great is that the dog food?"

The takeaway delivery chap is unfazed and probably now keen to leave, simply replies, "You can give it to them if you want, I just deliver it, mate!"

All done in good humour and at the required two metres apart. Thankfully the hordes of neighbours weren't passing by this week but it's been stressful.

I don't think I'm hungry any more… yeah right!

Day 21: Sunday 12ᵗʰ April

21 – the lockdown has officially come of age. Traditionally it would get the key of the door, which is ironic given we can't go out. How doubly annoying.

So, what to do on Easter Sunday? Go to church? After my school years at the convent when all the celebrations were built up to, talked about, rehearsed, finally celebrated, only to immediately be followed by starting the whole cycle again for the next one, I've had my fill.

Well apart from Christmas and everyone knows I'm mad on that one.

Easter though? Could take it or leave it. Except you do get a good long weekend. But all the days are feeling the same, so even that's a bit rubbish!

But to my shame James sends me a lovely cute Easter e-card. It's got Easter bunnies and eggs and flowers, really lovely from the charmer himself, James.

So, what to do? I'm struggling a bit to be honest and when I get dressed, I lie on the bed declaring to Shaun "I'm pointless, purposeless and sad".

My tears start. The wailing hasn't started yet but give it time…

I'm also feeling a bit weird about the boys not coming home to me tonight. They're normally with me on a Sunday night which means I have the aim of getting the house looking nice, shopping for the week ahead and generally nest building.

Nothing for it. Go out on my bike.

I do a 12 mile tour to myself trying out different routes so that later in the year when the traffic levels are back up, I'll know what I'm doing.

I go down to the Quayside where the seagulls have completely taken over the whole space under the Tyne Bridge. The noise (and the smell) is incredible. Good for them. I reckon the wildlife will just start to take over, long may it continue. I had seen on social media this week that the city CCTV had picked up footage of a deer wandering around in some sort of end of the world epic. Glad I hadn't brought the dogs.

I get home and watch some crappy TV while catching up with my "campaign knitting". Nice and pleasant way to spend a few hours.

Finally, I went to bed early with a glass of wine. Total anarchy, boomer style!

Week 4

Day 22: Monday 13th April

Stay Home: Protect the NHS: Save Lives

That's the strap-line that appears whenever the Government do their briefings. However, in a rare turn of events, it's due to be that rarest of things, bank holiday and lovely weather. People are going to amass in the parks and on the beaches, aren't they?

So, to counteract the risk, it's been changed to STAY AT HOME AT EASTER – catchy!

That is exactly what we intend to do. Stay at home. Again. But this time at Easter! You can't beat a bit of variety.

Shaun and I decide to both go on the morning dog walk which is our little break of the rules, being out together and all with the knowledge that one of us will have to go back out later. It will be the only rule breaking today but we feel like middle aged rebels none the same so that's fun.

We walk up the bridlepath as there are gangs of hi-vis chaps working on the flipping golf course, what's all that about? Take the day off fellas. And they weren't two metres apart as one worked and the other one watched... closely. I suppose even a pandemic can't change some habits of lifetimes.

We get to the field and elect to go through the woods, running the usual risk of the dogs chasing after a deer. We don't have to wait long. They disappear in the worst direction, the direction of the road. They can be away for twenty minutes and if you were the worrying type, you could imagine that they would hurt themselves somewhere and be lying waiting for you to find them, which you couldn't, and it would be awful. Welcome to my worrying mind.

My racing imagination of doom is quietened when Spike comes into sight after a few minutes and not long after that we see Arthur on his way back.

Except he stops short and we go to investigate. Oh yes, he's managed to get himself onto the other side of a skanky, manky deep burn. In truth it's more of a ditch but let's call it a burn to make it sound picturesque.

We call him over on the assumption that he had managed to leap over the gap once. We realise that it must have taken the speed of the deer chase to get him to clear the gap on his outward journey. This time he jumps but plummets into the decomposing, compost, shit mud. Right up to his armpits.

He thrashes about a bit and we're immediately spooked by the thought of him drowning in what is effectively black quicksand.

He can't climb up the sheer bank on our side, so he goes back.

Bloody hell, it's now terrifying. I go down stream to see if I can get across. No. I try to do that twice because as everyone knows, doing something repeatedly has the reassuring feeling of at least trying.

Finally, Shaun decides to climb across on a couple of branches. He goes to get suitable bridge building material while I repeatedly tell Arthur "stay, good boy, just stay". Seems to work and Spike sits with me, shivering and looking equally concerned.

What doesn't work, however, is Shaun's makeshift bridge.

The branches don't look secure, and I do actually think Shaun has underestimated his bulk. This small collection of branches masquerading as a bridge would struggle to support Nadia Comaneci. His confidence in his construction ability is high, though, so off he goes.

What unfolds in the next few minutes is one of the funniest things I have ever seen – only regret? No phone because the hilarious disaster was pure comedy gold!

He reaches the magic three quarter point, also known as the point of no return, and starts to wobble. Trying to recover himself he flails his arms around and commences the bend back, bend forward manoeuvre which is always the sign of impending doom. He grabs a branch that is still attached to the tree, it breaks. He flails a bit more and in what I swear was slow motion, falls into the black muck in a miracle dismount of feet first.

Maybe he was channelling Nadia Comaneci!

The black oozing muck immediately goes over his wellies. Swearing ensues.

After scrabbling up the other side he gets an enthusiastic hero's welcome from Arthur. He still has to deal with the sludge filled wellies, so he sits on a log and while fending off Arthur's appreciative whippet kisses, he tries to get the boots off.

They are securely suctioned to his feet, and in what is now top comedy moment, number two, he straightens his leg upwards to drain out the offending contents. Now, everyone knows that if you invert something which is full of liquid, the runny material will drain in a downward direction. The physics is lost on Shaun at this point, so on straightening his leg in the air the full contents went down the way towards an, up to this point, dry backside. Swearing ensues again.

We get home and don't have to worry about people staying two metres away from us – boy the stuff covering Arthur and Shaun is absolutely stinking.

Shaun goes to spray Arthur down in the back garden and Arthur proceeds to look so cold and sad that I carry him up to the shower for a warm shampoo. Good Lord that black smelly sludge is also really sticky. I tuck Arthur under a blanket and make Shaun a cup of tea. Both are traumatised and slightly in the huff with each other.

I take myself off for a bike ride to allow them to recuperate while I chuckle most of the way round, replaying the hilarious morning scene. Happy days.

Whippet Wordery - Spike

Arthur can jump brilliantly. He jumps onto the kitchen work bench to see what he can find to eat. Sometimes when The Family are out he just does it for fun and to annoy the cat.

He jumped over a big ditch today and I knew I couldn't make it so went back to human Mum. Arthur got stuck and it was a lot scary. Human Dad can't jump but he can fall and also he can shout.

I think we are both in the bad books and Arthur says not to worry and that they always get over it but I do worry. When we got home I was sick on the kitchen floor because my tummy knots up when there is a bad mood.

Human Mum mopped it up and tucked me in under a blanket. She just laughed. She's laughed a lot this morning so that's nice.

Day 23: Tuesday 14th April

Day 23 in lockdown and even though it's "lockdown light" compared to other countries, it's still getting rough.

I'm saying that because we are likely to have another three of four weeks of this and that means we may not even be halfway.

I have a meeting in my diary for this Friday and I'll need to change it to a Zoom call. No hardship there you may rightly say, but I remember making that appointment quite early on in the crisis and I was totally convinced that we would be "back to normal" by now. We're not of course, not by a long way.

The other reason it's rough for me is that the boys aren't around. When you first have a baby, they are quite rightly all-consuming, then they continue to be hard work on the domestic chores front but at all times, are great fun.

When it becomes less about tending to their every need (although I still seem to spend a lot of time embroiled in "need tending") they are damn great company. Well, my two are in any case, maybe I'm biased!

It's a long haul, this lockdown. We are, on the one hand, safe and comfortable but on the other hand there is an underlying threat and a very real worry for you, your loved ones and let's face it everyone.

If this fudging thing doesn't signal a move towards greater humanity, what will?

Let's leave today on that note. We got through it today and tragically over 700 people in the UK did not.

Day 24: Wednesday 15th April

Day 24 – 24 is not a special number for birthdays or any anniversary but I feel that I've turned a corner.

First of all, I had a boost yesterday when I got my head back into work. I had two coaching sessions and both the young managers found it helpful; in truth I'm happiest when I'm helping someone.

Secondly, I had a chat with my friend Frances in Edinburgh in the evening and that's always a good thing for my mental health.

And finally, I had a half decent night's sleep.

So, I wake up with a more determined mindset and write "JFDI" on my notepad! Yes, I will just do it and I did!

I set up the company's YouTube channel, did lots of emails, had a committee meeting (I feel I don't need to write "virtual" on the meetings now?), reached out (as the youth say) to the team, pushed our Disney holiday back to 2021 which seems a long way off, did a chapter on my MOOC qualification on cycling infrastructure and called the boys, skipped tea and nearly finished my book for the book club.

All good.

And it was sunny. And I washed some of the bedding, so on top of all my achievements and steps forward, the most immediate one was that it was a good drying day! Eat your heart out Mrs Beeton.

Because the weather is so nice Shaun and I both go out for the evening dog walk.

Shaun had already taken them out in the morning, so he is running the risk of the KGB being informed about his double dose of approved exercise. But we do it anyway.

To be honest, he's really "pushing the envelope" today because he also went to Lidl for shopping and if someone audited our fridge and cupboards, you would know that we were not in dire need.

He came back with a real rarity though and that was a 24-roll pack of toilet roll!!

We end the day as toilet roll millionaires. Never take that last roll for granted. A lesson for life.

Day 25: Thursday 16ᵗʰ April

The recriminations have begun. On the news, on Twitter, in articles, during interviews and even in meetings, you can sense a change in tone.

We've gone from: "We're all in it together; we need to all play our part; let's get volunteers; how can I volunteer; let's deal with the immediate crisis; let's all clap for the NHS".

To: "The UK Government were too slow; look what New Zealand has done; the New Zealand politicians have taken a 20% salary reduction; look at the fatality rate in Ireland and they cancelled St Patrick's Day while at the same time we were still doing Cheltenham Gold Cup Week and allowing a Stereophonics concert to go ahead."

As well as the pointed mentions of "herd immunity should never have been a plan", Priti Patel has never said sorry for the lack of PPE for the NHS. In fact the statement that workers should "not waste their PPE" is a deplorable piece of victim blaming. The overarching feeling is that the Government should have planned better and should have acted more quickly.

So, the state of the nation done, what's in store in the Gosforth Gulag?

As it turns out I don't have too much that definitely needs doing but quite a lot that probably needs doing. You know that expression "if you want something doing, ask a busy person" yeah that, in reverse. I'm adrift.

I decide to drift along until such times as some external prompt gives me the deadline that I actually need in order to galvanise myself.

Shaun and I, in the afternoon, go into the office (me on the bike, Shaun in the car, bad Shaun) and it feels weird. At one point we're both typing away on the PCs and I have a sudden urge to be at home.

I elect to come home first. You could argue that I bailed early but I have our village book club this evening. Again it's "virtual". Face to face is so last year, darling.

The book club is lovely. You always learn something new. About the book, yes but also handy intel. For example, I now know of a local book company to use as an alternative to the "do they actually pay tax" machine of Amazon. I also now know where to get really good veg boxes delivered. To be fair I brought something to the party by informing the group that the local wine merchants and Enoteca, Carruthers and Kent are doing deliveries. I think that was the best news of the night and a potential game changer in these trying times.

I felt I upheld my civic duty there.

Day 26: Friday 17th April

The Government announced last night that we are to be in lockdown for another three weeks.

In truth we knew this was coming so we'll just have to get on with it.

They're talking about a phased return so that might mean some businesses would be allowed to re-open. The problem with that is that staff have been furloughed in three week chunks and it takes time to get supply chains back up and running. The likes of Greggs would take about two weeks to gear up and if we were to have a "second wave" it would be a big financial hit for no gain. It's not as easy as it looks on paper.

That means that businesses aren't putting pressure on the Government, so in some respects there's no rush.

What I wonder is, as the majority of cases are still in London, why don't they just leave London on lockdown and allow cities in the North to re-open. This would mean we could economically catch up! There is always chat about "levelling up" but it doesn't seem to happen even after all that Northern Powerhouse chatter.

In my little, tiny business, I actually have quite a lot of work on. So much for thinking that one of the main issues of lockdown was going to be learning how to kill time! I'm not getting any income for the work right enough but keeping going and helping clients is going to need to be the focus.

I crack on and get finished for 4:30pm when Shaun and I walk the dogs together on the now repurposed community space that used to be the golf course.

We have a social appointment this evening!

We have received a "Gin-vite" from our next-door neighbours which is going to involve us sitting in our separate back gardens drinking gin and tonics BUT we're going to open the adjoining gate. Genius.

Ooooh a proper night out. Except it's freezing. I'm alright with my big puffa coat which the boys call my "posh football manager's coat!" Our neighbour should get one as the poor soul keeps having to go back in the house to get another jacket until he ends up with about six layers on and is still freezing. Well until such times as he's on to his third gin – central heating for adults and much better than Ready Brek!

We have a lovely few drinks and it's brilliant to talk to people "live" and not via a computer screen. After all this has calmed down, I reckon that opticians will be busy because we'll all have flipping eye strain after hours at the screen!

We can't let our two households of dogs mingle though as they'll just run riot and there are some suggestions in the press that you can catch the virus by patting other people's dogs.

We can't help but pat the new puppy from next door, Pepper. In true spaniel style she is very "busy" so she evades any attempt to keep her on her side of the garden. We have our doors firmly closed and with us playing with another pooch, our two hounds go their absolute dinger! They quieten down eventually and just stare at us through the glass doors doing their best whippet mournful faces.

We come in eventually, mainly to allow Simon and Lucy to make the kids their tea. We watch the worst film in the world and Shaun falls asleep.

With Shaun totally zonked out on the sofa and the two dogs gently purring away, I pour a glass of wine and watch the final two episodes of MasterChef. Marvellous Friday night that. A little bit more roll than rock but pretty good.

Day 27: Saturday 18th April

Day 27 of "the virus". I wonder what it will be referred to in the future. You know, in the same way as the "flu of 1957" is well known. The "virus of 2020" perhaps or just "COVID-19". The name is from the year it started unlike the notion uttered by someone on the TV who said, "well how did they get rid of the first 18"? We're doomed.

I have a birthday party to go to today! Not an actual outing of course but rather a Zoom call to celebrate my friend Janis' birthday. We are required to dress up though so that's exciting and something to look forward to.

For now, it's time to get out on my bike. I've finally decided on a name for it – Isobell. See what I did there? Isobell and I are off to the vets to pick up the dogs' tablets. Can't put dog worming on hold can you and it's an excuse for an outing.

The vet is closed! Shut at 11am not 12 noon as I was informed by Shaun. Ah well, he will just need to go on Monday. That'll teach him for just saying what he thought the time should be.

As I was already out with Isobell, I decide that I'd do an hour-long tour and that will be my exercise for the day. This will be an attempt to stay fit and fend off the flab being brought to me courtesy of the ever increasing wine and snacking habit, as well as the weekly takeaway tradition which has well and truly taken hold!

I have a great tour of Killingworth, Forest Hall, Wallsend and Heaton. Thirteen and a half miles and I only call one driver a dickhead so that's not too bad.

At one point I stop at a crossing and a mum and little girl catch me up on the shared path. The little girl gets to the lights first, only to be shrilled at by her mum "Stay back! Watch out! Stay away from the woman!". I didn't think I was foaming at the mouth and am lost for words. We are definitely now not going to have to bother with "stranger danger" because parents like that lady are successfully putting the shits up their kids about all humans.

I don't seem to do much for the rest of the day, but I do really. I ring the boys, do a bit of gardening, make a nice late lunch and take the dogs for a walk. Pretty much the usual stuff and all with nice weather so all good.

All this pottering around means I end up getting ready for the party in a bit of a rush. How can I manage to nearly be late? In my own home. I can't use the usual excuses of the taxi being late and the like. I literally only have myself to blame.

Anyway, I make it and I'm at my laptop with frock on, hair up, make up done and Prosecco poured. Unfortunately, I also have to have my glasses on otherwise everyone would be a blur so that makes the effort of applying eye make up a bit of a waste of time.

What a lovely chat we all have. Just shows you, it doesn't matter the setting, when you are in great company, you can chat for hours. Happy lockdown birthday Janis.

Day 28: Sunday 19ᵗʰ April

Remember I said that the recriminations had started? Well now they have been joined by revelations.

The news item doing the rounds is that our esteemed leader had missed COBRA meetings in February. Maybe he didn't think that the virus was much of a threat or he had better things to do. Really?

The death toll yesterday was 888. Alongside the harrowing daily figure, the other main story was PPE for the NHS or more accurately, the lack of it. Apparently, some nurses are using it too quickly, the victim blaming is continuing, that's helpful.

Back at the ranch, our headline is "Hoorah". Hoorah, the boys are coming back. Hoorah, we get to watch Race Across the World together. Hoorah, it's Indian Take Away night. So quite literally, three cheers for Sunday!

Shaun and I offer to drive up to pick up the boys, just as an excuse to go out in the car. We are all being discouraged from making unnecessary journeys but if we get stopped by the "feds" we've got a valid excuse, so we're all set.

It feels strange being out on the open road and somehow, I start to feel a bit anxious. I get panicky at the speed we're going on the A1. Not fast at all as Shaun is driving and his nickname is "Driving Miss Daisy" after all but it feels fast. Also, the open space of the main road and the expanse of Northumberland hills is a bit overwhelming. What's all that about?

It's absolutely brilliant to see the boys. I'm sure Archie has grown, and both boys' hair and beards have definitely sprouted.

We get them home and it's lovely to catch up with them, sitting in the sun in the kitchen having a beer and waiting for the takeaway. A curry and a beer! That's a winning formula.

Our huge banquet of food arrives except they've forgotten to put my main course in. We make a start while mine is getting brought over, with extra papadums by way of an apology. They didn't need to do that and there is no way I would get annoyed. These things happen and I'm completely and utterly happy in my little world with my boys back.

We have our feast while catching up with Race Across the World. Absolute bliss and how Sundays should be. All the Gosforth Fam back together scoffing and laughing at the telly.

Week 5

Day 29: Monday 20th April

It's the last day of the school holidays. Both boys have had an email from the school to say that online learning will start tomorrow.

Archie is pretty relaxed about it but the politest way I can frame James' reaction would be to say he is "perplexed".

"What's the bloody point" is the exact expression he uses. He's right and in actual fact there's a rumour that if the school encourage any additional work at this stage, they could fall foul of the slightly sketchy rules from OFQUAL. This threat could lead to the exam grades being reduced as a compensatory action.

Let's see what they request him to do and he can refuse.

For the last day of this slightly surreal holiday, I decide I'm going to be totally off as well. I'm not sitting behind my laptop when I could be chatting, watching telly and being out on my bike – the holy trinity of a good day off!

To get us through the next few days of family life, I have to get us some more provisions. Sadly, I have to go to Asda as we need cat food. Whilst us humans like everything from Lidl, including (perhaps especially) the in-store bakery, the cat would turn up his nose at anything other than Felix and Go Cat. Snobby little sod.

I get to Asda and take my place in the Russian style queue. It's not as long as the last time but it still snakes round the makeshift crowd management set up of trolleys tied together. I sense the maintenance of this new arrangement is already on the way out as the trolleys are more "strewn haphazardly" than in an organised arrangement.

The queue isn't too bad and keeps moving. So much for the "one person per trolley" rule though. Families are making a bit of a trip out of it, I suppose there's nowhere else to go.

I saw one couple with a little toddler (in the COVID infested trolley) take up their position in the queue with everyone giving them a good old British stare of disapproval. Have they not read the memo about shopping on your own.

The Asda KGB chap (all supermarkets have security now) comes up the line (at a safe distance of over 2m) and signals for them to come forward.

As the couple strut by, the chap gives out a stage whisper of "Great, VIP treatment, this is the way to jump the queue, we're priority customers". The Brit stare of disapproval and outrage reaches epic proportions. I think I also hear a tut. Well done, we showed them.

I notice a couple of things. One, judging by the look on the SS officer's face, they are not being considered VIPs. Two, I don't see them in Asda.

I sincerely hope that the strut up to the front was followed by "one person, one trolley" and they took off in the huff.

I do my circuit of the shop, complying with the one-way system. I seem to be in the minority but to be fair the arrows that had been taped down early on are degrading to the point that they are hard to see.

I did do my civic duty by pointing out the one-way system to an older chap who promptly continues to ignore it.

James has a quiz night tonight, 8pm in his room over the internet with his pals.

So, off he goes to "socialise", April 2020 style and we start our final day of the holidays also in true April 2020 style by gathering in the TV room to watch a film.

James appears just as we've finished the film "Town Like Alice" which was my choice as I remember enjoying it twenty years ago. I'd watched it in Australia on a bus ride to Alice Springs. What's the chances?

The details are sketchy but come flooding back while watching. However, the happy ending (spoiler alert) had somewhat masked my memory of how relentlessly grim the film actually was. Still good though despite me telling Archie and Shaun at the start that it was a "nice" film. Mmmm, mis-selling right there.

James says he wants to watch a film, but it is a school night (sort of) so I encourage him to go to bed. There are not many seventeen year-olds you can effectively send to bed but James is one of them. I won't have any of that influence if and when he does get to University this year, so I might as well make the most of it.

Day 30: Tuesday 21ˢᵗ April

Day 30 of house arrest which is a month's prison sentence in anyone's book.

The news on the radio is that parliament is going to reconvene today after the Easter Break. They aren't all launching themselves back into the cramped chamber though as they're only letting a maximum of 50 MP's in the actual house and others will join via Zoom, taking the total up to 120.

Wow, Zoom could stop the world from functioning and/or hold the world to ransom like some sort of COVID Bond villain!

So, the House of Commons will have some functioning but without the heckling and the tactical "bobbing" that normally goes on. What a strange little place it is with the practice of bobbing up and down in your seat, with no intention of asking a question or making any contribution but with the sole intention of putting the speaker off.

Good! They won't have any opportunity for schoolboy pranks. About time they grew up. If they start any nonsense presumably the speaker can just mute them. Now that's a good addition and beats shouting "order, order" to no effect.

The House of Lords is also starting today but fully digital. The interviewer on Radio 4 asked about the decision to be fully online and their speaker didn't really answer but I'm guessing it's because all the members are old enough to be in the vulnerable, shielding category.

Parliamentary scrutiny can begin and that's what it's all about. Having some sort of robust debate to sort out priorities, make decisions, discuss and agree bills and generally have a good process of governing.

823 deaths yesterday bringing the UK total of direct fatalities to 17,337. How awful.

In our little world we have Tuesday Afternoon Tea to look forward to. That's a good prison meal I reckon.

Due to the shortage of flour I've bought some scones and a cake so there isn't a great deal to do... or is there? I realise I've forgotten to get pork pies so we will need a quick trip to a shop. The minute that news gets out there's a full list. White bread (usually not allowed), beef slices for beef and stilton sandwiches which Archie had remembered having last year when we had gone out for afternoon tea for James' birthday. Ooh remember when we used to go out to places?

Now that we've got onto a conversation around "fancy sandwiches", there is a request for smoked salmon and cucumber. I check the fridge but the cucumber lurking in the salad drawer is officially manky. How annoying, I hate throwing out food and I was doing so well in this lockdown catering challenge. At least I can compost it which softens the blow.

Chocolate is the final item to mysteriously appear on the list. Chocolate is required for afternoon tea apparently. To get the shopping, James and I decide to walk to Lidl.

We have a lovely walk and a very productive shop including... drum roll... flour. Well, I've bought scones and cakes now so I'm not changing my plans but I get some for the cupboard anyway. This is how stockpiling starts.

We are officially part of the problem.

Day 31: Wednesday 22nd April

Day 31 of COVID clamp down and it feels as though this is now normal.

People have started using the awful expression "new normal" and maybe they are right. Maybe we have stopped peddling the idea that there will be a moment "when it's all over" and maybe this is indeed "it".

Our "new normal" is that Shaun and I get up and do a very naughty (and habit forming) watch of the telly in the TV room with a coffee. It really is a lovely morning room on these sunny starts to days. I try to get the boys up so we can get back to café opening times. The boys just make it before the shutters are up on the café kitchen. We have a lovely little breakfast with James having half a grapefruit, Archie and I porridge and Shaun… a ham and cheese sandwich! Each to their own.

With James having no schoolwork he gets on with his chores starting with the unpleasant but just slightly addictive task of weeding the front drive.

Archie and I knuckle down to our work and Shaun continues with a weird painting that he has started in an attempt to keep himself away from the TV and watching Donald Trump on YouTube. I still can't watch the news with him as it sends him into a downward spiral of worry fuelled depression with flashes of anger to add flavour. What roller coasters in hell will be like.

We "meet up" for lunch and the weather is so nice that we eat outside in the garden. The dogs come out to sit with us and to have an opportunistic nosey around at the low table. Arthur (of course, it's always Arthur) is slightly more bold than Spike and it takes some doing to push him away. They look like skinny wee things but when food is involved Arthur becomes a ton weight and seems to manage to turn up gravity.

We go our separate ways again until Archie is finished his schoolwork for the day and him and I go out on the bikes.

What a great ride we have, 13.5 miles up to Weetslade and along Reivers Way. There are a few people around taking their daily exercise, some are clearly well used to doing this sort of thing whereas others look like exercise newbies.

There is another mum on a bike with her son (not me, I'm not doing that weird thing of talking about myself in the third person!) who is even more of a wobbly cyclist than I am. Good for her getting out on the bike and hopefully getting her confidence up.

There is a mother and adult daughter with velvet tracksuits and full make up doing some sort of power walk as if they were in LA. Very glamorous and something I am definitely not achieving as I puff my way into the head wind, grabbing a hankie from my pocket every now and again to deal with the inevitable runny nose. It's all glamour.

We get back safe and sound and I crack on making tea. Beef stew or to give it it's full title "hearty beef stew". I make more than the "hearty portions for a family of four" in the recipe and of course there are zero leftovers.

My days seem to revolve round mealtimes which is fine except I feel full all the time while the chaps are constantly on the search for "scran".

Chatting to friends and judging by comments on social media everyone is a bit the same and reporting weight gain. Ah well that'll be the next crisis, but it'll have to wait.

Day 32: Thursday 23ʳᵈ April

At 5pm every day there's a Government briefing on the BBC. Last night the medical chap Professor Chris Whitty said that the virus is not going to go away, it won't just disappear, and a vaccine is a long way off. That'll be that then.

This morning the news is dominated by the reports of the first human trials of a vaccine which are starting today. The people being interviewed are careful to say that it's a long process so we still need to adhere to the rules of social distancing and basically stick to the rules of stay at home, protect the NHS and save lives.

The news is also focussing on the advice around the wearing of face masks and the consensus seems to be that a face mask won't stop you contracting the virus but it may stop you passing it on to others.

I'm just not sure about it. This may be my imagination but the people who are currently choosing to wear the masks (thank you by the way) seem to be the ones who wander more closely to others. They may actually get distracted by the mask because my observation (not scientific) is that a higher proportion of mask wearers walk out into the cycle lanes. The masks may be a great idea but to be honest it's not going to help either of us if I hit you at 15 miles an hour, love!

So, Professor Whitty, how can we make sure that mask wearing doesn't turn us all into little masked up liabilities? We might have to practice wearing them so we don't feel like a bit of fabric is magically going to stop anything bad happening to us.

I go out with James on the bikes today and have a great 15 mile jaunt in an attempt to stave off the lockdown lard.

By contrast and not helping at all, this evening Shaun and I have a little drinks date with some friends, via Zoom.

One of our friends has been alleviating her full shielding boredom and keeping her fitness up by creating a little golf area in her garden. Genius! She grabs her iPad and takes us on a golf course tour which is fraught with technical challenges, somehow even funnier when the camerawoman is in her seventies. Shouting into the iPad, she delivers a great running commentary but falls short of some demo shots.

We find out that other friends have a Dad in hospital with the virus but he is not yet on oxygen and another's sister is very ill. What an awful time and again we remember just how lucky we are and how dangerous this situation is for everyone.

Let's get those masks on! Not for the first nor probably the last I say "let's just do what Chris Whitty says."

Day 33: Friday 24ᵗʰ April

Now that the furlough grant money has been extended to the end of June it feels like this is definitely going to be a marathon effort.

I'm up early and after coffee with Shaun in the TV room and an episode of the calming while still murderous Father Brown, I'm on a webinar at 8am run by a young woman from Australia all about how to launch a podcast programme. Why not. The webinar is really useful, so I sign up for her training and support package to get me started. Perhaps you can teach an old bird new tricks!

I have breakfast with the gang then on to the CBI daily webinar for an update but also to hear what the Shadow Chancellor of the Exchequer has to say. Here is a synopsis:

"So, what have the Government got wrong?"

"Blah, blah, NHS, blah, blah, PPE, blah, blah."

"What would Labour have done?"

"Ehrm… things differently."

"Like what?"

"Oh, things."

That's not exactly what was said but that's the general gist. With Parliament now open again, I had such high hopes that there would be a level of scrutiny and a modicum of insight into how things should have been handled. Even though we are all in "unprecedented" (yeuch) waters, there needs to be a challenge doesn't there? Isn't that what the whole system is built on?

Ah well.

It's Archie's turn for the "PE with Mum on the bike" treatment which is now part of our family curriculum. We decide to go into town and down to the Quayside. What a great ride and going over the Millennium Bridge was the absolute highlight of the week. There's nothing for us to do on the other side so we sit on the bench and have a drink of water.

We do 15 miles so good effort.

We see a lot of people adhering to social distancing and just as many who were not.

Coming back through the town is a bit odd. A real mix of abandoned shops, empty streets and then suddenly a really busy part near Northern Goldsmiths at Monument. Where the hell are all these people going and why didn't they get the two metre memo?

We get home for lunch and Shaun and James had braved Lidl so we have a bit of a feast of bacon, egg, tomatoes, sourdough bread and as a garnish... chicken pie. Can you tell that Shaun was in charge of the lunch menu?

We all get on with our projects with me doing emails, Archie doing schoolwork, Shaun doing his painting and James playing football manager.

Simon and Lucy next door send us a "Gin-vite" for 6:30pm which is a nice new habit that we are retaining.

After our big lunch Shaun and I aren't hungry so decide to skip tea but that won't work with teenagers, so I nudge them towards pizzas from the freezer. The pizzas were bought for an emergency and this is officially an emergency.

We decide to light the fire pit as Simon has donated some logs for our "night out" and remembering his freezing blue face from the last time, we feel we need to do something.

Of course, the fire starts off rubbish with it oscillating between pure hot flames when Shaun had squirted it with accelerant followed by no heat and just thick black billowing smoke. That'll please the neighbours. Ah well we have to put up with the constant noise of strimmers and lawnmowers and jet washers so they can deal with a bit of black acrid smoke on a nice evening. Oh dear now that I write that, it does seem to be a bit inequitable.

We have a lovely chat and it is really nice having the fire even if we still end up a bit cold. Just like the average living room in the 1970's, we're boiling on one side and freezing on the other. Oh and the other neighbours are probably plotting revenge strimming for 6am tomorrow morning. Cheers!

Day 34: Saturday 25ᵗʰ April

Over 20,000 people have died from the virus in the UK. It's both staggering and deeply sad.

Meanwhile, over the pond in the US, Donald Trump is causing a stir again.

When you read about what he says, you can't quite believe it and then when you watch the footage it's even worse. I saw the morning news and only a few seconds of his most recent performance at a press conference.

This is the gist of what he was saying: "the bug is very clever... light kills it, can we get light into the body... I'm not a medical man... but some light... that would work... or some disinfectant... inject that... get that right into the body"!

What?! Really?! Why don't people around him tell him to stop talking until he has a rational thought?

Of course, there will, as a consequence of this public service announcement be some people deep in Texas now drinking Cillit Bang, oh Lord.

Here in the UK the news is pretty much as it has been for a while. Lack of PPE for NHS workers, a death toll (I so hope we are not getting immune to that daily report), stories of people staying at home, and stories of people not staying at home.

Today there are some new statistics to mull over, delivered by Home Secretary Priti Patel. She has good news. Oh, go on then. In short, she is pleased to announce that shoplifting had gone down... eh?

Now let's think about this for a second... the shops are shut. They are actually closed.

Not for the first time through all of this do I utter the words "you couldn't flipping make it up"!

I was being updated on this "pleasing news" via last night's briefing, but I can only tolerate it for so long and have to switch off, both the TV and my own brain.

Back to my incubated little world of laughs, cuddles, films and of course food. Today is the much anticipated take away day.

We're doing the same Thai restaurant that Shaun and I had scoffed recently but when James and I prepare ourselves for the ordering process by trying to find it on Just Eat, it was nowhere to be found.

James has the idea of finding the phone number in my outgoing calls on my phone and then googling the number. Genius. But it got more complicated because there was no obvious number from last Saturday, so I have the brainwave of looking up my journals to get the exact date. It was two weeks ago. Wow, time is still flying. When this lockdown started the concern was how to fill time – it's still skimming by.

Anyway, we find it and finally find a menu online and everyone chooses. I go to ring the number and it comes up on my phone as a saved number! That would have been really handy if I'd also managed to remember the name of the place. For future reference its THAI CHANG. I'll need to remember that but just in case I have another memory fail, I ask the restaurant to pop a menu in with the order. They say they always do. Yes, you've guessed it, there's one in the takeaway menu drawer.

What a complete rigmarole but the food is safely now on its way which is always a great feeling.

James and I take the dogs for their walk and we decide to try the other side of the "dog walker reclaimed space" formerly known as the golf course. The trouble with the "other side" is that there's no gap to cut through the fence so we'll have to climb over the gate and lift the dogs.

This would all be fine but there are two problems. Firstly, Spike is unfeasibly heavy for a whippet and secondly when we do manage to get him off the ground, Arthur goes totally bonkers. For some reason seeing anyone lifted up (especially Spike) sends him into a complete frenzy. He leaps at you and tries to bite Spike, in fact the biting can continue even after poor Spike is back on terra firma.

We do Arthur first to practise and limber up! Arthur done, we brace ourselves for Spike and needing all spare hands for the chunky monkey, I tie Arthur to the gate. Arthur does indeed begin to lose it but the lead holds and we manage.

The whippet lifting procedure is a bit stressful for all involved but it's worth it to have a change of scenery.

Also, there are no other dog walkers on this side. You'd never get the big Labradors over that gate that's for sure.

The dogs have a great time especially when they chase a cat up a tree in some sort of classic cartoon manoeuvre. A final quick run around and a dig in pristine bunkers and we're ready to go home. Spike isn't. He sits down on the raised tee off area doing his best face of both stubbornness and pleading.

He comes along eventually at a very slow and slightly pointed pace and we go through the gate lifting procedure again. Mental note to selves: the gate nearest home is slightly higher. Good Lord, that is a workout!

When we get home, I do a little bit of curating of the book exchange so that people can see the titles without rummaging. It's just a plastic tub that I put out so that people can drop off and pick-up books - I fear there is more dropping off than picking up going on but it seems to be rising in popularity and usage.

Just as I was doing that the chap with the food arrives. I love that. It's like going to the loo in a restaurant and coming back to find that your food has appeared at your table. You feel excited, lucky and clever at timing all at once.

He tells me there's a menu in the bag. Not that clever then.

Whippet Wordery - Arthur

I love jumping up on things. It's the bestest thing ever because I can be all high and look The Family straight in the face. I also get lots of attention with shouts and laughs and cuddles. Sometimes it is an angry shout but not for long and as I always say "it's worth a shot."

I don't like Spike getting picked up though. It makes me feel weird having to look up at him while I'm down low on the ground.

Sometimes human parents of other small dogs pick them up when I go running up to say hello. It doesn't bother Spike and he says that I shouldn't be so FOMO. He says that a lot.

Day 35: Sunday 26th April

We're going to do a full exercise regime all day and scrub the house and get up to date with all our chores.

No, we're not. Today is "movie marathon day." Hoorah!

I leave the boys to sleep in, as it is the weekend after all. Or is it? All days seem to be roughly the same but I'm trying to carve out some differences on Saturdays and Sundays. I wonder if people who've been retired for years still do that. I wonder why it's important.

A few years ago friends of ours did a big European trip in their motorhome and they did try to differentiate weekdays from weekends, but I think that was just in an attempt not to drink a bottle of wine each day.

Today is the weekend, I keep telling myself, so that means a lie in and treats and wine. It'll be back to lockdown house rules tomorrow.

Much faffing around ensues during the day and whilst that's fun, it doesn't help to achieve a movie marathon. You have to be focused on executing your goals after all. People have been reporting using lockdown to learn Mandarin and master multiple yoga poses while also redecorating their entire house. It's called "lockdown shaming" and I think it's probably best not to get involved.

We have goals too though and we are knuckling down and putting in the work. A few hours later our hard graft has paid off because we've munched through the popcorn made by Archie and have polished off The Verdict with Paul Newman, a film about Brian Clough's time at Leeds United (my choice which surprised the chaps) and Archie's choice of the full on Kurt Russell fest of Sky High. Kurt Russell as a superhero complete with a geeky son, high school fights and gadgets. Seriously, what's not to like?

Three films in limited time. That's an achievement in anyone's book. It may not qualify for any lockdown shaming but we reckon Joe Wicks would struggle with the commitment we've shown today.

Week 6

Day 36: Monday 27th April

Day 36 of what has now moved from "not a sprint but a marathon" past "ultra-marathon" to bloody "iron man"!

In the final episode of Blackadder Goes Forth or should I say the iconic final episode of Blackadder Goes Forth, Captain Darling joins them in the trenches just before they are about to go over the top. Blackadder in the comedy genius way that the name Darling provides asks "how are you Darling?". To which Captain Darling replies "not so well. I'd rather hoped to go back to work at Pratt & Sons, keep wicket for the Croydon Gentlemen, marry Doris. I made a note in my diary on the way here which simply said *bugger*".

I'm not drawing any great parallels here but was minded of that scene when I saw the kitchen calendar entry for today which simply said "Week 6. FFS"!

We are still in the trenches with no obvious nor certain end date. There are reports from Italy and Germany of further lockdown easing and the pictures of little children in Italy finally playing outside of their houses with their friends, albeit with masks on, is really cheering to see.

Our Government aren't committing to a transition plan and are still keeping us in the lockdown rules which are ok for us. We are doing ok. But it is hell for others, we know that.

At this point my attitude to work is… distant. Not in the "distance makes the heart grow fonder" kind of way, absolutely not. This becomes even clearer for me when I take Shaun on one of my Weetslade bike rides, the one when you go west for 15 miles or so.

Anyway, it strikes me that there are more cars on the road than last week. I keep saying to Shaun "where are they going? Are they ignoring lockdown? Are people just fed up now?". But actually, the panic in my quick fired, repeated questions is less to do with people having no sense of civic duty and more to do with me not wanting to go back to "normal".

I'm happy that my life has hit the pause button for a bit. I don't want to launch back into chasing after each weekend at the expense of weekdays; wishing away work months just so we can go on holiday, staring at the minutes ticking away when stuck in traffic knowing that I'm letting down people who also have better places to be.

No, I want to go on bike rides and cook and sit in the garden and play games and watch films and have the highlight of our week to be afternoon tea together.

Maybe we can work out a way to hold the gains but for now we have burgers for tea with sweet potato fries, so let's stay in the moment for another week.

James and I take the dogs out for their evening walk before James has his weekly quiz night with his pals. They each prepare a category and this week he has entertainment, so during our walk we run through his questions. The only one I get right straight away was "what's the longest running scripted TV show?". Answer: The Simpsons.

Perhaps as a direct result of his old Mum getting it so easily, he said he would probably replace it. None taken!

We walk the dogs round the golf course which is still reclaimed for dog walking and other recreational purposes. We just elect to do our usual side which doesn't involve any lifting of animals. We have a little bit of drama when we meet the two lovely huge black New Foundland/Labrador cross dogs. They are fluffy and are so massive that we call them the "bear dogs".

We love them. Arthur does not.

He is, in truth scared but tries to come across as brave by barking loudly, from a distance. He barks and barks while never leaving our side, even at points slyly hiding behind my legs. The "bear dogs" just quietly stare at this yappy little skinny thing, not reacting in the slightest.

We get home and have tea. James does his quiz complete with my suggested replacement question. "Jack Nicholson and Heath Ledger both won an Oscar for the same role, name the other two actors who achieved the same".

Ha, cool Mum points restored.

Answer: Robert De Niro and Marlon Brando playing the part of Vito Corleone. You're welcome.

Whippet Wordery - Arthur

I quite like other dogs. I love Lucy the whippet. Her and I like to run off really fast and Spike can't keep up. I feel a bit bad about that but I can't help myself. Lucy is great.

I saw the big black things again today. They get walked about as if they're dogs but they can't be. They're ginormous. They're very fluffy and you can't tell which end is which. I gave them a good shout today and I told them to "get lost." I don't think they heard though and how would I know, I might have been barking at the wrong end.

Day 37: Tuesday 28th April

The weather forecast is lovely again. The weather is definitely making this stay at home business much easier.

Shaun and I start the day in our usual way with a coffee and an episode of Father Brown. It's such a gentle series, even with all the violent deaths and family murders and arrests and thefts… very restful.

Off on the bikes again today, this time with James down to the Quayside. We scoot over the Millennium Bridge because it's fun and he hasn't done it yet then back over to the North side of the river and along to the West to see if the little Italian café that I had spotted a couple of trips ago is open. It is.

I go in for the coffees and in true Italian upselling style the owner asks if I'd like a glass of wine. "It is past 12", he says and there is no real persuasion needed so I get us two flat whites and two small reds. Oh, and a packet of crisps as they don't serve any other food until Thursday.

We sit on the bench outside and have a lovely chat. What a simple thing to do but now that we can't do it routinely, we seem to appreciate it even more. Time with the boys is so precious, I'm determined to enjoy it. On that note that's what I meant when I said to the boys that I probably wouldn't do work this week until they had gone to their Dad's. Seemed like a perfectly reasonable and nice sentiment. But that's not how I said it. I actually said "ach, I can just work all the hours on Thursday and Friday, I've got nothing else on."

This had the effect of making Shaun feel very unspecial. Oh dear, well done me.

Anyway, back to the Quayside. What a brilliant spot and a fantastic way to spend an hour or so but we have the hill climb to do so off we go back through the town and home. I didn't use the Turbo setting, honest.

We have cottage pie for tea, but we didn't have enough potatoes so this fact together with Shaun putting too much milk in the mash had the effect of the sludgy small amount of carbs sinking into the mince. It ended up being less pie and more a kind of grey mince and potato stew thing.

I have a little snooze in front of the TV. Well, why not. I also am very tired because I'm still getting up so dashed early. The boys put it down to Shaun and I being "boomers", remarking how ridiculous it is to get up at 6:30am. They think there's only one 6:30 in a day, although no doubt in a few short years they will find out that you can see 6.30am at the end of an all-night party! A phenomenon now very much in the rear view mirror for me.

I get my boomer revenge for all the ridicule by making them watch me looking up something on YouTube on the TV. It was very painful to watch apparently with cries of "do you want me to do it Mum" and "no don't press clear" and "oh you're in the wrong bit now".

Ha ha, that was fun and a nice piece of torture to remember.

Day 38: Wednesday 29th April

Day 38 of lockdown lunacy. I'm not saying that because I think what we're doing is madness, it's not, it seems to be very sensible. No, I'm saying it because it is driving us to the brink of madness.

It's making me feel a bit caged up and a bit anxious. Made worse by the fact that the boys are going to their Dad's this afternoon. Boo!

I mustn't be the only one concerned about mental health issues as that's the lead story on the morning news. A very anxious young mother of a tiny baby was featured, and the poor girl did indeed look at the end of her tether.

Another lady was talking about her work as a call taker for the Samaritans. That's an important service all of the time and especially now. The Samaritans get lots of calls around Christmas time when people have problems spending a couple of days at home with their family, so what must be happening now?

The death toll in the US continues to rise at an alarming rate. Apparently in the US the death toll is greater than in two decades of the Vietnam War. Still Trump struts about blaming China, calling for the lockdown to be stopped and generally saying he's handling it all brilliantly. The man is a bloody menace.

Back at home my car is getting returned today. I haven't missed it at all and it's strange to have it back on the drive, like a big useless garden ornament. Well, it'll be handy to store things in. Maybe I'll put the spare food provisions in there. The chaps will never think to look in the car boot for crisps!

Because I'm going to quarantine the car for 72 hours, we take the boys up to their Dad's in Shaun's mini. It's nice to have a run out, what a complete old boomer thing to say I realise.

It's less nice when Shaun gets lost exclaiming that I, "should have kept him right" and saying that he'd, "never been on this road," in his entire life in fact.

Apparently, someone born in the North East and who has spent the majority of their life here has never ever driven to Morpeth via the Cramlington Road. And what's more, it's clearly my fault and I'm not even from here originally.

Mild argument ensues. Bet the boys are looking forward to the peace and quiet at their Dad's. I ask them if that's the case and they say, "of course not." Lovely, polite, untruthful answer. Well done fellas.

But I'm nearly forgetting the big news of the day. Archie let me cut his hair with the clippers. He is very proud of his beautiful (his word) thatch of hair. We call it Grampa badger hair as it is very like my Dad's crowning glory. Such was the solidarity between the well covered pates that every time I remarked that it needed cut in front of my Dad he would say "don't listen son, it's great".

Archie is therefore protective of his inheritance but even for him it's getting outlandishly long. The bike helmet is starting to sit perched on top of it which I think is a safety consideration.

So, I was given permission and I went in. He'd washed it first to get all the gunky gel out so it's easier to comb, but wow there was even more of it than I thought. Ten minutes in with full clipper action and nothing much had seemed to happen. At the fifteen minute mark it all started falling around him. He seemed pretty relaxed about it but I'm not. I start saying the same things I'd said to James "there's only a couple of weeks between a good and bad haircut" and "it'll grow in in no time". Shaun says it isn't helping.

Quick closer trim round the ears and we are done. Not too bad. Not that well styled but once he got some gel on, he seems ok about it. Phew! The barbers are going to be busy when lockdown is lifted, that's for sure.

Not too bad a day at all. In fact, this new way of life has lots and lots going for it. Maybe if I just stopped watching the news, I could pretend I didn't know when we were allowed to go back to normal. You know, like the theory that there are people dotted around remote parts of the world who don't know the war has ended.

That'll be me next year when I'm still staying at home, protecting the NHS and saving lives.

Day 39: Thursday 30th April

I start doing my backlog of work on the laptop, catching up with emails and doing some finance admin. All good and great to get stuff out of the way but my heart's not in it.

Then I get a call from the boys' Dad and I completely panic. What's happened to one of the boys? Have they developed a fever? Too early to have fallen off a bike, I reckon as James probably isn't even out of bed.

It's none of those things but still not good news. The University of Glasgow has retracted James' offer of a place. What? How can they do this when the A-level results aren't even out yet. So much for the assurances in the news.

James is understandably upset as he's built his whole vision of University around his first choice of Glasgow. He did the extra law test required, he's chosen his accommodation, he's planned his trips to Edinburgh to see friends studying there and of course he has the whole Macnaughton clan in Glasgow lined up for Sunday lunches.

I make some reassuring statements, but it sounds like Mr Black at the school is doing a good job of giving practical advice. I end the call with a reminder that, whilst this is bad news, it was nothing compared to what went through my head when I saw the number come up on my phone. Angus appreciates that and says that he'll text a "nothing to really worry about" message before any future calls.

A little bit of research later and we find out that Universities have been given an instruction by Government not to fill up places with UK students. It would appear that with less overseas students coming and less money in the Treasury coffers, the domestic students have to be spread out amongst the institutions. So this next part of James' life is also going to be affected by the damn virus.

I have a little text conversation with James and he seems OK but I can tell he's very sad and I wish he was here.

Shaun and I decide that work can bloody well wait, and we get the bikes out to get some exercise and fresh air and to check out the food offer at the little Italian café on the Quayside.

It's brilliant. Shaun has pizza and I have a ham panini. A couple of glasses (well cardboard cups) of red wine and we felt we were on a weekend city break.

We get home and open a bottle of Prosecco. The house rules have completely gone out of the window but we're not hurting anyone, and it is day one in a ten day stretch of the boys being away. That's my excuse anyway.

Day 40: Friday 1st May 2020

For 40 days and 40 nights we've been doing some sort of penance. That's sounding a bit biblical, so we'll leave it there.

The bike is getting picked up for its 100-mile service and I had great intentions of getting out for a ride beforehand, but no chance.

Once it goes, I knuckle down to work, but I can't muster up any enthusiasm. I pull myself round a bit and respond to emails. I'm alright when I get my head into it but despite getting into a good flow I do have to stop because we have a Zoom Cocktail Party to attend!

We don't do well with my glass of wine and Shaun's Jack Daniels and coke but watching everyone else, I now have three recipes for cocktails that I will endeavour to make sometime in the future:

Firstly, from the Savoy cocktail book: double Canadian Club; 25mls Vermouth; Bitters. Seems simple enough.

From our friend Vincent we have the French 75. Apparently named after a field gun used by the French in World War I, which in a stark similarity to this cocktail had the reputation of blowing your head off: 1 tablespoon of lemon juice; 1 teaspoon of sugar syrup; double gin; shake and pour before topping off with champagne.

Finally, a gimlet, which seemed to just consist of sugar syrup, wine and gin which is shaken and topped off with bitters. If you add egg white you get a gin sour. That can't be too hard.

As bitters are used quite a bit, we get into a discussion about the Angostura bitters label which has always been strangely too big for the bottle. Apparently, the story goes that it was an enterprise by two brothers, and one made the bottle while the other designed the label. They were not on good terms and just pressed on with the two parts of the endeavour in splendid separateness. But when they came together for the finished product, it didn't work. As our friend told us this tale of woe, I resisted the temptation to mumble "typical bloody men". Zoom doesn't really lend itself to a stage whisper or a quip I have discovered.

Now that I'm writing the recipes, I could actually turn onto the idea of cocktails but that would mean getting the ingredients in. Wine is easier but that's hardly the spirit, see what I did there?!

First Zoom cocktail party report card: Audrey needs to do her homework and must try harder.

Day 41: Saturday 2nd May 2020

Another weekend which feels exactly the same as a weekday. This is not what retirement will feel like as my retirement vision is to be in Malta and go scuba diving every day. You never know, when all this is over, I might just bloody well accelerate that little vision for my future self.

But today we are still locked up under house arrest. There's a rumour that Greggs is reopening on Monday! I've only heard it via Archie but when it comes to food outlets, he's usually clued up, so you never know, it may signal the easing of the lockdown.

But today we are off on a bike ride to the coast. I pack the sandwiches in my wee bike panniers along with banana bread and lashings of ginger beer. Actually it was water but I went with The Famous Five Do Lockdown for a moment there.

Off we go via the Weetslade Reivers Way, over the cycle paths and round the treacherous A19 roundabout. We hit a brutal headwind, but I carry on as I am so desperate to see my beloved North Sea. It's the tonic for my soul.

We make it and I just stop short of a few tears as we sit on the little metal seats looking out at all the big ships which just seem to hang in the water like enormous ornaments.

After our sarnies, we decide to head home but a different way. I didn't make the outward journey sound appealing, did I? And in truth it is quite unpleasant in parts.

We scoot along the sea front which has those ridiculous shared pavement and cycle ways. They do not work at all well, in my opinion. They probably work for cyclists who don't care about being a nuisance to pedestrians, but Shaun says I even ring the bell in an apologetic way.

We go on the road for a bit which is hazardous with cars driven by boy racer types and older drivers who are keen to overtake you and then go slower than the bike. What's all that about?

We make it to the safety and joy of another Waggonway, this time Hadrian's Way and it's brilliant to scoot along taking in all the blossom, the birdsong and the lovely weather. Cue the Famous Five theme tune right there!

If you are down at the river front, you just know there are hills ahead of you to get back inland. The hills at Byker are pretty steep so I elect to go onto the full Turbo setting. I therefore have to wait at the top for Shaun to catch up.

Now, Shaun can be pretty loud, a trait which he denies but it is a fact, and it can cause problems. Today was one of those situations. He puffed up the hill towards me and in full hearing of the residents of the area who were out and about he exclaimed "you know some parts of Byker are alright. I mean I wouldn't live here but they're surprisingly ok."

I jump back on my bike and in the spirit of the old joke about not having to outrun the tiger but just outrun your friend, I'm off!

We get home feeling like we've "earned our tea" so we order mixed grills from the kebab shop, I can feel the meat sweats coming on already.

The food arrives and as with social distancing the delivery driver leaves it on the step. Good Lord, I can hardly lift the bag. I reassure myself that the driver doesn't know there's only two of us and I manage to get the bags back in the house before any neighbours go by.

It was really good, and I finish mine at about the same time as Shaun is putting the last piece in his mouth. Noticing this exclaims "wow you must have been hungry, must have been all that sea air". No Shaun, this was half of mine, the other half is in the fridge for lunch tomorrow. This concept of leftovers is still a struggle for him. I'm not sure it will ever take off in his world.

Day 42: Sunday 3rd May 2020

The Government is starting to say that the lockdown measures have worked and we're getting "past the worst".

That's what is being said during the official briefings and by the Conservative MPs but other parties are putting forward their perspective, which is more pessimistic and damning.

There is also still the issue of incorrect or no PPE for front line workers and now the testing is going out to a big prime contractor. There's a smell about money going to people who have all been to University with the people who hold the budgets. I wonder how this will all unfold.

Back at the ranch, I'm not going to say anything about today because it was depressing. I was sad and grumpy and upset, and it was all a bit rubbish.

The boys not coming home on a Sunday night is the worst.

Whippet Wordery - Arthur

My human Mum was lying face down on the bed today. She had her outside clothes on so I knew it wasn't "lets go to bed" time. I wasn't sure what was going on.

I got on the big bed with her, which is normally a right treat but today it wasn't fun somehow. She didn't say anything, but her hand twitched a bit, for a strokey pat on my back and a twiddle of my ear. So that was nice. I just waited. A lot of whippet work is just waiting.

Week 7

Day 43: Monday 4th May 2020

This just got real. BBC Radio 4 has run out of episodes of The Archers. What the actual?!

It's also Star Wars day. May the 4th be with you and all that. So, taking into account both of those things I write a strange combo in my work diary: "this crap just got real, get a grip".

It seems to do the trick because, with resolve, I get cracking on with work things.

Shaun has a worse day. It starts with the morning dog walk. I knew something was amiss when there was a knock at the door and standing there was Spike.

No, he's not quite that clever. He was with Carol and Will, also known as Lucy the whippet's Mum and Dad. They said they'd found him down at the bridge, just wandering and looking distressed.

I ring Shaun to tell him that Spike was safely at home but looking unhappy. I got the full sorry tale when Shaun and an equally forlorn looking Arthur come back, and it goes like this:

Walk in the woods, spots deer, deer gets chased onto the golf course, golf course official starts shouting at Shaun, dogs come back, accusations of being a poacher levied at Shaun, more shouting from both sides now, whippets scared, Shaun furious, golf guy is called names. Spike can't take it and runs home.

This dog walking trauma is followed by a frustrating time for Shaun trying to edit a training video. He's having a hard day

All I can do are three things. First, crack on with my work and house jobs although Spike has had a trauma vomit in his bed so the jobs are backing up – ah the joys of whippet ownership.

Second, look after Spike as he is staying within three inches of me the entire time. I've put his bed right next to my work chair but the minute I move he's there. I can't even nip to the loo without him accompanying me. It's like having a toddler.

Third, keep Shaun fed. We get to about 1:15pm and he's still staring at the PC. Well, I assume that's what he's doing, it's very quiet in there. So, I make him a sandwich and slide it onto the desk in front of him.

Later I make a cottage pie and things seem a bit brighter.

The dogs are still in his bad books, but I think I'm ok.

Whippet Wordery - Arthur

I bloody love chasing deer. They're a great bunch of fellas and go really fast.
Spike can't keep up really and he doesn't like the shouting that happens afterwards. I don't mind. The

human parents seem to get over it so all in all it's worth it, I think.

I don't like the man in the yellow vest thing though. He shouts at human Dad and that makes human Dad more madderer. I'm in trouble today but human Mum took me and Spike in the kitchen and gave us a treat. She told us it was a secret and we were to be good all day. I can do that.

Day 44: Tuesday 5th May 2020

We all thought at the start of this that the lockdown would be for two weeks. We are now a month overdue.

I decide I'd better re-engage with the Government briefings in case they're saying something more than:

"Well done to everyone in our beloved NHS (please don't mention that along with my colleagues I personally voted against your pay rise a mere few months ago)."

"Well done the Great British Public you're all doing your bit (I've never been to the North but I hear it's lovely this time of year)."

"We're doing marvellously well, and the healthcare workers all have lots and lots of lovely PPE (until last month I only knew that expression in reference to my PPE degree from Cambridge. You know the one, the one where you learn all that clever political and economic theory, don't use it though, must dash, have a country to run don't you know)."

"Thank you for listening, I hope that reassures you all. Now where do we get a decent meal now that the damn Carlton Club is closed, gosh we're all making sacrifices right, left and centre. Oh no, strike that last bit, there is no centre ground. I'm losing it, are you sure the Carlton Club is still closed?"

End of briefing and now to the weather, what's in store for us today Carol?

Yeah that. I'd decided to duck out of listening for a few days to protect my mental health.

So, I catch up and last night's was headed up by Michael Gove. I fear the worst and he doesn't disappoint. He tells us the daily death toll is 315 which is getting less but still alarming. The total is an awful 28,446, a staggeringly heart-breaking figure to even try to comprehend.

He tries to sound sincere and then moves on to Ramadan and how people won't be able to break their fast with friends and family. That is definitely worth acknowledging but he then goes into some sort of game of "inclusivity bingo" and starts reeling off religious ceremonies topping off with a general sweep up of weddings, christenings and funerals. Very bizarre.

I don't think it was worth watching. I get on with some work and have a pretty good day of knuckling down.

Later we're off to Waitrose in Ponteland to get the wines for a wine tasting we have booked on Thursday. I'm not totally convinced that this counts as a "necessary journey", so the devil only knows what we're going to say if we get stopped by the Feds. I road test a response in my head while Shaun drives at his favourite 34 mph in a 60 mph zone: "Oh officer, you see they just don't have the range of fine wines in the Jesmond Waitrose, I did try there first. Also we've already decided, if they don't have the ones we want in

Ponteland, we are absolutely not going to do the additional journey to the big one at Hexham. We're all making necessary adjustments, you see officer. What age are you? Does your Mum know you're out on your own?" It'll be fine.

We make it and as the policy is one person per trolley or household, I elect to go in. Fifteen minutes later and the wine is secured, very good.

You know how when you chat to people from your hometown you revert back to a stronger accent? Well, what I was faced with when I came out of the small supermarket was a very loud Shaun talking on the phone to one of his oldest friends, Carl. He was literally standing in the car park shouting down his phone "well aye man, we're at that Waitrose to git wine like. We're git posh ya kna, like". Followed by "aw, ye kna me, Carl, mate, ah divvent kna oot aboot wine, like".

Oh Lord, ground swallow me up.

And of course, we still have to get into the mini which is festooned with union flags, like some sort of Brexit mobile.

Just as well those crack security guards were pre-occupied with their phones as we left, we'd probably be barred. It's git posh in Ponteland like.

Day 45: Wednesday 6th May 2020

Full day at work which was pretty productive. Shaun is off out to get cocktail ingredients at Rehills, which is the corner shop in Jesmond with the best booze collection in the county. Then he goes to our friend Vincent's butcher shop for dog food.

He's also going to drop off wine for Vincent as we had done our community bit by getting their order for the wine tasting. There. We have reduced car journeys and done our bit, see young officer, we are almost key delivery workers.

Not much to report today. Lots of work done, booze cabinet full of ingredients for cocktails (I have done my homework, I'm all prepared and ready for the next test) and the freezer is full of dog food.

Shaun got a couple of nice steaks from Vincent and some sausages. Vincent had put in extra and we've discovered that the amount extra you get is in direct correlation with how much his boss has annoyed him that day. Luckily for us she had been on form recently.

I had a nice little catch-up phone call with Frances in the evening. We thought it would be about an hour but ended up being about three hours which allowed me the opportunity to make a good start on the Mount Gay rum that Shaun had just procured. Ooh we're almost in Barbados. Doesn't scan that does it but it's the closest we're going to get.

Day 46: Thursday 7th May 2020

Day 46 in the Big Brother house. "Audrey come to the Diary Room."

"Have you seen how much Mount Gay rum has been consumed during a supposed 'nightcap' with Frances?"

Oh dear. Not to worry, I had a great chat and feel fine. To be fair I never get hangovers. Perhaps if I did, I would drink less. Not to worry.

What's in store today? Couple of calls, lots of emails and then the long-awaited wine tasting.

Let's jump to that as the work stuff is not that interesting for the reader. I like it though and seem to have my work mojo back.

We end up nearly being late for the 6:00pm start. Shaun had every intention of having a shower and changing out of his scruffy gear. Do remember that Shaun's scruffy gear is very, very scruffy and often also very, very smelly. I know they can't smell him over Zoom, but we have to sit reasonably close in order to both be captured on camera. His pungency better not affect my enjoyment of the "fine bouquet of the wine" that's for sure.

But he ran out of time so simply with a minute to spare, he stuck a shirt on top of his t-shirt. He still has the tragic manky joggers on the bottom half when he joins me at the screen, with me muttering "standards, dear boy", and "we're only ever a mere seventy-two hours away from anarchy remember."

The wine tasting was fun from beginning to end. What a hilarious and eccentrically smashing group of people we know and now that we're Zooming rather than meeting in person, we're seeing another side to everyone.

The free version of Zoom only gives you forty minutes so it was over before we knew it. We were immediately called by Vincent and Sinead to carry on the wine and chat and get the full story as to why Vincent was late arriving home for the call and why Sinead was not joining in with the wine tasting at the start.

Apparently, the wine that Shaun had dropped off yesterday was left at the butcher's shop by mistake overnight. Vincent's boss had spotted it and put it in the industrial fridge. Vincent got it out this morning but it was near frozen, so he stuck it under a bush near his car to thaw out. Eh? And then forgot to bring it home. He had to go back to get it and was late back, complete with room temperature white wine. That all explained Sinead's facial expressions throughout. Comedy gold. Poor Vincent.

Day 47: Friday 8th May 2020

Day 47 but more importantly it's the VE Day bank holiday.

It's the 75th anniversary of VE Day which is so important and something that I've been looking forward to since the Government announced the move of the bank holiday.

I was, along with a large number of people up and down the country, thinking of bunting, dressing up, a street party, baking scones, Dame Vera Lynn, sunshine and champagne.

Well, we've had to adapt those plans. We've ordered afternoon tea to be delivered which is just as well because there are currently no eggs in the supermarket. Ooh it's just like in the war! Not really but the analogies are coming thick and fast this week.

I watch a bit of the morning news while I try to finish knitting my red, white and blue bunting. I say bunting, to be honest it's more of a scarf but it's the best I've got without going to the shops and they've likely run out by now.

The breakfast news can be hellish to watch as the interviewing "roving reporters" can be really clunky. This morning was delightfully no exception.

The wandering reporter had gone into a care home and was interviewing a war veteran resident, Charles. What a complete gent. Even in the face of some awkwardly worded questions, he remained gentle and polite. With every answer he added "and also hopefully we'll come out of this with more respect and kindness for each other".

We notice that there's another old chap in the background, the TV camera just picking him up through a door to what looked like a kitchen or restroom.

This fellow looked more of a staunch military man, military cap, medals, straight back and presumably fantastically shiny shoes although we couldn't see for sure. Why wasn't he wheeled out for our viewing pleasure? We decide that this old boy perhaps wouldn't have been as polite in his answers, dismissing any analogy drawn between the war and this crisis. For dramatic fun, we play out a few scenarios such as:

Interviewer: "People are saying that it was a similar experience in the war to now?"

Old Chap: "Bugger off. Do you get shot at going to Asda? No, you don't."

Interviewer: "People missing their families though, that's the same?"

Old chap: "It's been six weeks! I never saw my wife for four years and by the time I did she had a 2-year-old son. We just got on with it!"

Shouting alternative stories at the telly is one of our favourite pastimes but that finished for now we're off out to walk the dogs.

Anyone who knows me knows I'm a stickler for the two-minute silence. The moment when the whole country stops, and together, is bound in time thinking about others is both moving and uplifting.

So, when I realise that we're going to be out in the field still on the walk at 11:00am, we have to get organised. Shaun finds BBC1 on his phone so all we need now is a suitable place to sit. We find a wee bit of thistle free grass which is perfect. The Royal correspondent Nicholas Witchell (also known as "that bloody man" after Prince Charles was caught calling him that at a press conference about 20 years ago) is still on about the royal family.

Now at this point I glance at my watch.

"That's weird" I say, "it's 11.01am on my watch. Why is he still banging on about the Queen?"

Enter the strange world of Shaun.

Wait for it…

He uttered the words that I never thought I would ever hear: "oh I paused it a couple of minutes ago, so yeah it's probably after 11 now."

Who the flip pauses a live broadcast with a critical time element when an entire country joins together to do something? What the actual?

I'm apoplectic. So, I get up and as calmly as possible continue the dog walk.

I decide to do my own 2-minute silence but in truth it's probably a good five minutes before I can utter any civil words.

Respect and kindness said Charles this morning. Respect and kindness, I repeat, respect and kindness.

Day 48: Saturday 9th May 2020

Day 48 of the lockdown measures and it's looking like the Government's handling of the crisis is going to pivot into a complete debacle.

There had been a SAGE (Scientific Advisory Group for Emergencies) meeting this week and the Scottish and Welsh responses had been in tandem with the message that full lockdown measures were to remain in place, unchanged. As you were, people of Scotland and Wales. Do carry on.

Johnson's response was to whet the appetite with a statement along the lines of "big announcement on Sunday". I don't know if the Downing Street discussions had included any words along the lines of "next phase" or "easing of lockdown" but by the time the weekend papers had been set to print the story was very much "phew, it's all over".

Despite there being an ongoing crisis with daily fatalities still around a shocking 600 and despite us now being aware that care homes have been, and continue to struggle dealing with the escalating situation, the speculation is still that "we're done"!

There is a further teaser starting to leak out in the TV reporting and that is the new banner "STAY ALERT"!

"Stay at home, protect the NHS, save lives" seemed to be doing ok so why do we now need to be alert in our own homes? We'll have to wait and see but the clear messaging seems to be unravelling.

On the home front, it's a glorious day so we're off for a cycle ride to the Quayside. I'm under no illusions that today's bike ride must not be a 32-mile epic. How do I know that? Because Shaun keeps chanting "not 32 miles" as we get ready. I fear he is still saddle sore after our coastal trip last weekend.

We explore Hadrian's Way a bit more and it's brilliant. All industrial and smelling of the sea, just what a river route should be.

We stay alert and get home, thus saving lives.

Day 49: Sunday 10th May 2020

Day 49 and today is the day that we find out the new instructions on how we, the Great English Public, need to go about our lives. We will find out how we can "do our bit", in an alert fashion presumably?

I forget about that for now though as the weather has taken a nasty cold turn so Shaun and I decide to have a second cup of coffee in front of our morning TV indulgence. We go complete rock and roll and watch two episodes of Father Brown.

I've mentioned the theory before that any society is only ever 72 hours away from anarchy and it's this type of reckless behaviour which will tip the country over the edge!

We reign in our wild ways and have a day of pottering before we set off to go and get the chaps. The real big-ticket event of the day!

It's so great to see them and they're on chipper form. James has been building a PC and is bringing it to the big city to get an expert to sort out a little problem. In reality we're taking it to a wee guy he's found in Gosforth but a much needed expert none the same.

We get everything and everyone packed into the car with James holding his PC (precious cargo) on his knee. As we set off the car seat belt alarm sounds. Assuming the cargo wasn't stored securely, I stop and make them check everything. All seems fine so I start to get out so I can go round and "check my bloody self". It turns out I don't have my seatbelt on. I'm always a little bit excited to see the boys, that's my excuse, I'm not a forgetful boomer, honest.

We get home to full on further excitement from the dogs, they really love to see the boys and it must seem like ages for them. Cat nowhere to be seen. Takeaway ordered and I can relish that moment of knowing a feast is on its way and we can fill the gap comfortably with the family life of dog walking, table setting and central heating tinkering.

Great evening but I'm quickly shattered. I'm blaming the two Father Browns, it's too much for me.

Week 8

Day 50: Monday 11th May 2020

Day 50 of lockdown but now the whole nation is confused. Here is a summary of Johnson's briefing at 7:00pm last night:

"Well done the Great British People".

"If you can't work from home, we urge you now, from tomorrow to go to work."

"From Wednesday you can go out for unlimited exercise".

"You can also meet another person outside, providing you are two metres apart."

"The 'R' is between 0.5 and 0.9 and we may be going into phase two, so we can be more flexible".

"But be alert."

"We urge you to go to work but don't use public transport. Use your car. Or walk or cycle."

"Well done."

Where the absolute flying fudge do I start? Twitter overnight has gone bonkers, not least of all the advice to use your car ahead of any active travel options. It's been well reported that there was a danger of a "car led recovery" and this would be bad news for our already air polluted island and especially in the midst of a pulmonary virus pandemic.

But I'll start with this small rant if I may:

It's 7:00pm on a Sunday night, you out of touch Etonian throwback. How are people going to know if they need to rock up at work tomorrow and if they don't turn up, will their employer say that they've missed a shift?

And because you have now said it, will you, in two weeks time, tell the Treasury to stop furlough from midnight on the 10th of May?

You see, you, ego-filled pillow of a man, the Great British Public

1. thinks through practicalities,
2. will now worry, and
3. has been on the rough end of this kind of thing before.

This whole briefing is filled with flaws, can you not recognise that? Can you?

Can you see the red ball, children? Boris can't.

So, with the Dad's Army quote of "we're doomed" running through my head, I set about the working day with a little less vigour than perhaps would have done it justice.

Not to worry the chaps are here and we're all safe and well. The only thing which is a little bit in my control.

In the evening James goes off to his room for a quiz with his mates while Archie, Shaun and I join another quiz. It's Pete's Lovely Online Quiz, live from London and courtesy of an introduction from my friend Frances.

This week's topic is "drink". I reassure Archie that it will also include soft drinks, tea and coffee and general questions like songs that mention drinks, such is the format from Pete.

Of course, Archie renders my "let's be inclusive to the kid" ramblings slightly obsolete when he correctly pipes up "Jägermeister" for an early question and "Jack Daniels" in the picture round. Both questions which had Shaun and I stumped.

On the general knowledge round, we are shamed further by not listening to Archie when he says that Turkey is the only country in Europe which doesn't celebrate Christmas.

Shaun had distracted us by a suggestion that it was Kazakhstan. He does try to get in a story about him working there in most conversations to be fair so I should have dismissed it and gone with the little chap.

I quip that everyone knows turkeys don't vote for Christmas and get rewarded with a groan. Tough crowd!

I only get perplexed looks when I try another with "and goodness knows who voted for our turkeys in Whitehall". I blame the audience darling, I was marvellous. Time for bed.

Day 51: Tuesday 12th May 2020

Day 51 of the new "eased lockdown" where I fear people will use the confused messages as an excuse to do exactly as they please.

For us we're going to stick together and do what we need to do and no more. But we have things to do today, as we're in the final preparation for James' 18th birthday tomorrow.

This includes Archie getting James a card. Which sounds shoddily last minute, but he has diligently been in receipt of a series of deliveries into the house, all secreted away into his room. I only know of one of them which is the drinking helmet - you know the one where you put cans in the side and drink through a tube. Both classy and funny!

We all get on with stuff in the morning including James and I going on a trip in the car to drop off the PC (precious cargo) at the repair place.

The journey is weird because I haven't driven for six weeks, so it feels totally alien. The strangeness continues at the repair shop as there was a full procedure to go through. The process is to wait at the entrance and ring up to the first floor so that the guy can come to the top of the stairs and shout down further instructions. The further instructions are basically filling in a book and leaving the hardware in a designated plastic box.

All seems fair but the chap is not only an entire flight of stairs away but he is also in a full bio suit. He looks like he is dressed up for chemical warfare not to sort out a snag in Windows 10. I ask. You wouldn't expect anything less, now would you?

Apparently, he does lots of work for doctors' surgeries, so he needs to be ultra-careful. That makes sense but if I was him, I would also enjoy dressing up, pretending to be a spaceman.

James had elected to have a Chinese take away for his birthday tea, but as we are now fully in the routine of regular takeaways, it didn't seem special enough. I didn't want to dissuade him but offer to do his favourite of steak and chips with homemade peppercorn sauce. He bit my hand off, not literally.

So, we scoot up to my friend's Charlotte the Butchers for four juicy rib eyes and in a "while we're at it" kind of way we also come away with eggs, a chicken and a gammon joint, so we're set for the week.

We finish off our little jaunt out with a trip to Lidl for veg, fruit, milk, crisps and Prosecco. That's the 5 a day that everyone needs during this challenging time!

Later I nip out for a bike ride with Archie because we need our exercise and he still needs a brother birthday card. I suggest we go to the "big Sainsburys" which causes confusion between us until I realise that the supermarket you normally term as "big" is the huge one that requires a car. Now that I am predominantly a cyclist, I had changed my perspective and meant the one on the high street. Big enough. Perhaps we all need to reign in our idea of "go big or go home"?

As you do on bikes that you don't want stolen, we take it in turns going into the shop with Archie going first. He comes out with a great "best brother" card, complete with birthday badge. He's made the mistake that we all have though, and not collected the envelope. I suppose at least card manufacturers have responded to environmental worries by stopping putting the card and envelope in a plastic cover. On my turn to go in for a couple of things, I pick up the envelope. I'm not sure how I'm going to explain the seeming theft of a random envelope but luckily I am unchallenged.

Film choice tonight is mine. Not that my name was picked out of the "film choice hat" but rather because I said I deserved it. My rationale was that 18 years ago today I was in labour with James and in excruciating pain. They hastily agree that I can choose, perhaps just so that I didn't go into any further gory details. That's a winning strategy.

The Brosnan version of Thomas Crown Affair it is then. Hoorah!! Cue the music and shouting "ooh spot the briefcase under the bench". Spoiler.

Day 52: Wednesday 13th May 2020

Day 52 of lockdown, new rules style, and from now we can have unlimited exercise outside.

It's hard to imagine that this had previously been something that we'd taken so much for granted. It's two months exactly since Shaun and I had our little day trip to Hexham. Carefree and chatting away to each other on the train, wandering around the town, tourist trip into the Abbey complete with a visit to the crypt with total strangers squashed in together. Lunch in the French restaurant, a few drinks in a pub and a busy train ride back to Newcastle. A situation which is now totally alien to us.

How amazing to think that a mere two months can reset what you view as normal, acceptable and socially responsible.

But for today the outside world can go and fly a kite (approved activity) because it's James' 18th and that's what the whole day is going to be about.

We've all taken the day off and it's going to revolve around fun, food, pressies and chilling together.

There's a moment when we have to wait to see if Archie has any live lessons. He doesn't, so I get the pancakes on and the day can begin. I encourage (badger) James to open his cards. Bless him, he would have waited but it's too exciting (I'm too excited).

In the middle of the card opening there's a knock at the door. Is it Paula with the surprise cake? No. Is it Paddy with the surprise bike? No. It's Simon next door with the surprise beers!

We get the pancakes finished but before all the dishes are done Shaun takes a call from his friend Carl. He sneaks off into the TV room, so he doesn't disturb us. Disturb us? He shouts so loudly down the phone you would be able to hear him in the next street never mind in the kitchen. I step in when the conversation turns a bluer tinge as they share stories from their glory days!

The door goes again: a Cadburys chocolate hamper courtesy of Linda. Another knock soon after and this time it is Paula with the cake.. An amazing film reel complete with an extra cake on the side shaped as a box of popcorn. It's so realistic that Shaun helps himself to some Butterkist before he realises.

The cake delivery concluded; we go out for a dog walk all together. Ooh what a treat!

We risk going into the wood. That makes it sound like it's scary and haunted but it's just the risk of the dogs spotting deer and being gone for half an hour on an adrenaline fuelled chase. They spot deer.

As they jet off at full speed, we do the usual futile shouting but there's no point to it really, so we give up.

We spot some other deer on the opposite side of the path and Shaun says, "Oh Lord if they come back and spot them they'll be off again". Guess what?

I spot Arthur making chase and give him a shout along the lines of "come here you sodding little shit-stick". And he comes back! It's not until we set off again along the path that I realised there was a mum and a little girl nearby. Ah well she knows a few new words now. Every day's a school day and you don't get that kind of earthy stuff on the national curriculum!

When we get home a parcel has arrived and as is the norm now it's been left in the glass caddy (the bottle caddy of shame as I like to call it) in the blue wheelie bin. It's the 18th birthday party balloons so in a very "non-surprise way" we blow them up while James looks on.

We have a little bit of snackage for lunch and afterwards, spurred on by one of James' presents from Shaun, his first good malt whisky, we have an impromptu drinks tasting session. We start with the Mount Gay rum. I pour some in a shot glass for us all to try a sip each but Archie goes first and necks it. We then try some of the bourbon as a comparison. I duck out of that one as bourbon is horrible stuff, in my humble opinion. Shaun gets more carried away and gets out the absinthe.

Again, I don't try it because firstly it's disgusting and secondly, it's a hallucinogenic. I'm bad enough with normal alcohol. The boys are unfazed and try it. Cue the gagging sounds. Well, it is an 18th birthday party after all and maybe a bit of rocket fuel does elevate a lockdown birthday.

We continue living life on the edge with a few games of poker using James' new set. I start off with a reasonable hand but as I rejoice in my win, that first round was hastily classified as "a teaching round". Of course it was fellas!

We have a few more rounds with Shaun confusing himself and "betting like a child" as his poker playing friend used to say to him. We play the strange rule of "all chips in" for the final round and the birthday boy wins, which seems about right.

Steak, peppercorn sauce and sweet potato fries followed by a film and some of the malt whisky. Not a bad 18th birthday all round. He'll have plenty of opportunity to celebrate with his mates, we hope anyway.

This virus will have to be "lived with" as the latest saying goes, but surely we'll get some of our old lives back. Otherwise with none of the youth socialising I fear the population will plummet. Best leave the journal there for the day!

Day 53: Thursday 14th May 2020

Day 53 of living with the virus and back to work after our lovely day off.

I promised Archie a cycle into town and a pizza at the little Italian café on the Quayside. So we do a small amount of work and then set off so we can get there before it closes.

We have a nice cycle into town and once there, we make for the picturesque and steep Grey Street. I'd promised Archie we would scoot down at a pace. But no, there are roadworks. The new cycle lane is going in and as I'm a bit of a stickler for not riding on pavements it means that we have to get off and walk.

We ride fast down the next bit which is Dean Street and is even steeper. But it's slightly terrifying as I have a fear of tipping over the handlebars and/or hitting a pothole in the road. There are lots of those, aren't there Newcastle City Council?!

At the bottom, Archie declares that we could have gone faster. Not on my watch fella. Stay alert!

We make our way along the cycleway to the café and I notice there aren't as many walkers as there had been on previous excursions. I can't help wondering if people have got fed up with the instruction to get daily exercise or whether now that it is no longer limited to one hour per day, somehow they aren't making the effort to "get their dues".

We get to the little café and Archie secures our bench while I go in to procure the promised and much awaited pizza.

But what's this? They're only doing small pizzas? Nothing for it, I order two for Archie as well as a coke and for Mum a panini and a cup of red wine.

We sit having a "restaurant meal" on the park bench and it is absolutely brilliant. We have a lovely chat about all sorts and it's a moment in time that I'll never forget.

Of course, as with all trips to the Quayside what goes down must come up. So, we will need to steel ourselves to do the homeward journey. I'm alright as I have the pensioner Turbo setting on my e-bike but Archie will need every ounce of the pizzas for energy. On Shaun's old bike with the fat tyres, I think the pizza ride today is definitely going to be calorie neutral.

We decide to avoid the uphill for a bit longer by going a bit further along Hadrian's Way, and I can also show Archie the route to the coast. This is a mistake as I fail in my navigation and we end up being a bit lost in Walker (not what you want to be fair) and what I didn't know but had suspected, Archie's football shorts were not the best on a bike.

I've broken him.

The cycle ride had been a game of two halves: lovely, brilliant and then awful and a bit sorry for itself. We'd had our half time though and something better than pie and Bovril. I mention this little analogy as we walk up a big hill near home. I don't get a laugh.

Day 54: Friday 15th May 2020

Day 54 and the next round of confusing advice is out from the Government. They've developed a graphic to illustrate the risk ratings which is a 1-5 "heat map". This is being likened to the Nando's sauce ratings and apparently, we need to be "lemon & herb" before we can mix again.

We are, however, "very hot chilli", you know the one in the black bottle that you don't touch at Nando's unless you're a psychopath? Shaun likes that one, so let's not discuss that further.

We therefore have to avoid meeting up with friends. But we can go out with members of our own household. And we can go to the shops but stay two metres apart.

This can be confusing, so I decide to doodle a few scenarios to help my understanding. Firstly, what would happen if I was to go out on my own to the shops and was of course surrounded by strangers, hopefully staying the required two metres apart. Yes, all allowed. Do carry on.

Next, what about if I meet my friend Paula for a walk. Still allowed, stay two metres apart and be alert.

Finally, what about if I am with James on a walk and I happen upon my friend Paula. Not allowed. Disperse. Disperse!

And there you have it. You can be "in the company of strangers" but do not bump into anyone you know. Disperse, disperse!! Stay alert! Go home!

But that's all academic because we're not going anywhere today. Archie and I have work to do so we get stuck in and rather than allowing James and Shaun to feel aimless (also known as not allowing them to enjoy themselves) I give them a list of chores.

Shaun attacks the big window cleaning with gusto and James does his bit by doing the hoovering. Well half doing the hoovering as it keeps getting stuck on the rug, sucking up the corners which causes James to be totally perplexed and defeated. I eventually send him off to do the stairs as I can't concentrate with the various noises and questions. Watching teenagers tackle practical jobs is not good for your mental health or family relationships.

I have my final Zoom meeting at 4pm which is exactly the same time that Shaun starts his home gym routine. Whilst I've got used to timing the mute button so that the grunting noises are not picked up by my fellow meeting attendees, today there is an added risk of Shaun's shirtless frame coming into view via the mirror in the dining room. I really should move that or do what they do in films and smear it with Vaseline to shade out the detail. For now, I just move the laptop.

Not for the first time do I mutter the Virginia Woolf quote, "room of one's own and £500 per year."

I get finished work and James and I go off for a bike ride to Jesmond Dene. The Dene is busy with quite a few young lads playing football so presumably they are from the same household? Yeah right.

There's a bit of chat about "don't worry about the cooking Mum, we can just get a takeaway" but too late I've already put the gammon joint in the slow cooker. The recipe I got from my friend Lynn said to cook in ginger ale but we couldn't get any, so I've gone rogue with Irn Bru or to be totally accurate the non branded "Ironbrew" from Lidl.

It looks odd and smells a bit unusual. There's a deep suspicion in the ranks but actually it isn't totally inedible.

To round off with another Woolf quote: *One cannot think well, love well, sleep well, if one has not dined well.* Perhaps I should have caved in and got the takeaway.

Day 55: Saturday 16th May 2020

Day 55 of the new measures which are exactly the same as the old measures except people are confused. We are cutting through the confusion by staying at home, and staying alert!

Today is the weekend and even though it could feel exactly the same as weekdays I try to make it special by letting the boys lie in and by making pancakes.

We have no ham for the savoury ones, so I cook some bacon and also the mushrooms that need using up.

This is a bad move as everyone liked the new ingredient mix. I must stop making improvements to my pancake repertoire. It's already a full menu production. That's the last of the flour though so for now, I'm saved by the shortages!

Archie and I are off on a cycle ride to Weetslade and then westbound along Reivers Way. We go as far as the path takes you until you reach the scary main road. Being alert we do the sensible thing and turn back.

On the return journey we explore down another track which takes us to the runway approach to Newcastle Airport. That must be quite a sight when planes are hurtling towards the ground over your head. Today there are no planes as they are all grounded which must be a relief for the ponies in the fields nearby.

There's a reasonable hill up to the runway area which has just been topped up with gravel. Pretty unhelpful for bikes. I spot it and manage to get myself out of the tyre ruts and onto the higher grass middle. Archie has a harder time and at one point is doing the cartoonish action of peddling and not getting anywhere. We get to the top and there are a group of guys drinking cans of beer and smoking floral smelling cigarettes. Archie and I scoot by and I manage not to tut anything about rules, not being from the same household and it being 11am.

As we turn to go back, we have a chat about the floral smelling cigarette gang and also the dangers of the downward slope of "gravel hill". We decide I will go first so that I can do my disarming old biddy greeting of "alright fellas" which usually stops any heckling and as for the hill, the plan is that we will avoid the tyre grooves.

We hadn't figured on two things. Firstly, Archie not being able to help himself and try to do a thrill-seeking overtaking manoeuvre. Secondly, a cyclist coming up the hill.

The two incidents come at once resulting in me being shoved into a gravel filled trap. I plough into the gravel and come to a complete stop but manage to narrowly avoid a somersault.

Archie just laughed, as did the "floral cigarette gang". I do a long-awaited old lady tut as I try to regain some dignity.

We make our way back and I pop into the shop for essentials: milk, tonic water, Coca Cola and flour.

Still no flour. Result!

Whippet Wordery - Spike

We love ham.
Human Mum says it weird that we can hear
the fridge opening lots of times but as soon
as the ham is out we are there. It's the only time that me
and Arthur and the cat stand together. To be fair the cat
is on his top spot on the kitchen worktop but we stand
patiently together staring, waiting for our little bit.
The pancakes were on the go today but no ham. What's
all that about? There's something weird going on but I
don't know what it is. We had to make do with cheese
and human Mum said we were all making sacrifices.
That's weird as well.

Day 56: Sunday 17th May 2020

Day 56 and it's getting a bit busier out there. The golfers are back. I figure that's a measure to stop marriages crumbling or retired couples from perhaps killing each other. But for us it means that the relaxed dog walking is over.

We have a lovely morning. We're all on various devices, together and apart at the same time in a kind of throwback to an internet café. I mention my observation and get a perplexed look from the boys.

James is playing football manager, Archie is doing some quiz thing and Shaun is "being creative" by making movie posters with the head of the actor replaced by that of an animal. You know the type of thing, a bloodhound face on The Godfather. He didn't take on my suggestion to change the title to The Dogfather so I think he's missing a trick there.

I get us lunch using the newfound technique of keeping a bag of chips from the takeaway and doing egg and chips in the oven. I don't get the expected "aw that's great", "thanks Mum". No. What I get is multiple requests of "ooh is there any of that soup that you're having", "can I have avocado?", "is there any of the gammon left?"

Needless to say, I get grumpy. I pull myself together because it's just not that important and we only have another couple of hours together. Actually, that is another factor that I realise notches up the level of angsty grumpiness.

The boys get all packed up to go to their Dads. They're pretty efficient at living between their city abode and their country residence as I breezily term it to make it sound like an advantageous thing. In this arrangement over the years there has also been the added benefit of two birthdays, so we better get the birthday boy delivered.

They're away for a week which seems much less painful than the previous 10 day stretch. "See you next Sunday" is psychologically more manageable. I resolve to use the time that they are away to do lots of work and not drink wine. Let's see how that works out shall we?

Week 9

Day 57: Monday 18th May 2020

This is now feeling like our new way of life.

Even after the "easing" of lockdown rules last week, we're all still in a bit of a limbo state. Those people who are going to work are, in the main, the ones who have never stopped. There is talk of Greggs opening again which will be welcome, in the North East anyway as people need their steak bakes back on the menu.

I have a crap morning which extends into an awful day.

I get the shock news that one of my friends has passed away. She had cancer and now the world is less colourful and less vibrant by the untimely loss of a lovely, generous, funny lady.

There will be no funeral attendance where we could offer our support to her husband and family, perhaps helping by remembering happier times of trips together and of course their wedding which was amazing and feels shockingly recent.

Later we have our daily chat with the boys which is a tonic. The end of the day and the world somehow seems more dark and uncertain.

Day 58: Tuesday 19th May 2020

Day 58 of lockdown. I say lockdown but judging by the frigging traffic as I cycle up to the office to print stuff off, we are in the minority as dyed in the wool staying at home advocates.

I had the misfortune to tune into the 5:00pm briefing last night. It was led by Dominic Raab who has as much charisma as a beige Ford Mondeo left out in the rain on a drizzly Tuesday in February.

He put up the slide of the Nando's sauce spice rating and we are apparently still "hot chilli" (4) but maybe going to "mild chilli" (3) at some point. Still a way off "lemon and herb" so we need to do what we're doing for quite a bit longer.

I'm never going back to Nando's.

Day 59: Wednesday 20th May 2020

It's going to be a glorious day with the weather which is lovely although I'm a bit busy with various projects, both work and personal.

I spread all my work out on the dining room table. Something I've been trying not to do as:

1. I like us to eat at the table and,
2. I don't want to have the work constantly looking at me in an accusing manner.

But the spread out done, I can now see it all in one go and it doesn't feel as scary, albeit I know it's going to take a lot to get through it.

In the end I do my usual thing of getting into a good flow at a late hour in the day, I break off in the evening for our little village book club (over Zoom obvs) and then get back to it, finishing about 1:00am.

I feel better that I've got on top of things a bit. One sure foot in this shifting sand, one giant leap for womankind.

Day 60: Thursday 21st May 2020

Day 60 of austerity measures... oh sorry silly me, that was another way to tell us in the provinces that we are "all in it together", while the people making the decisions do what they want.

I say this because it turns out that the Tory hard-man Dominic Cummings has flouted the lockdown rules by reportedly driving his kids hundreds of miles to his septuagenarian parents. It's hard to know where to start with how wrong this is and it will, I fear, open the floodgates of "why should we bother".

But never mind what's going on in the Barnard Castle area, today is pizza Thursday!

It's amazing how far you get in a few minutes on a bike. We are in town and on the Quayside in no time. Shaun places our order in the Italian, I secure a bench outside and we call the boys for a little lunchtime catch up.

Shaun is his usual loud self and just as he utters the words "ha ha I probably shouldn't say this, it's not very PC", I hang up.

Archie sends a message saying "cold" and I reply that yes, I could be accused of a cold exit but I'm trying to make sure we don't get barred. If this lockdown is going to be with us all summer, this is the nearest thing we have to lunch out.

We munch away at our food and sip our cardboard cups of wine as if we're on holiday. A little mini break from lockdown, for at least a couple of hours.

Shaun decides we should take a bottle of wine home, which we do and therefore our holiday extends into the evening.

This lockdown is not helping with the alcohol consumption, but the alcohol consumption is helping with this lockdown.

Day 61: Friday 22nd May 2020

They say (you know, "they") that it takes a few weeks to change a habit and eight weeks to change the way your brain is wired. So, we're perhaps on the cusp of this being our new way of life. If I was being fancy, I would say a paradigm shift but that's maybe asking a lot from a 61 day stretch.

It has some benefits but there is a heavy toll and going into the future if it does change how we live permanently there are going to be consequences.

James and Archie wouldn't meet future partners, we wouldn't have enriching experiences like live arts performances, we wouldn't see other parts of the world, I wouldn't go scuba diving... what? Hold on.

This crap has taken a serious turn. Actually, I have air tanks in the garage filled with pre-COVID air – I'll just use them for as long as I can. Might get kitted up for my next trip to Asda. That should save lives.

Day 62: Saturday 23rd May 2020

Technically speaking today is the start of the May Bank Holiday weekend and the start of the boys' half term break. But as there are now no demarcation lines, I'm working all day.

Shaun is sympathetic to my plight in the "poor you" kind of way but I like my work and it would be nice to get up to date so I can take Monday off and enjoy the bank holiday / start of the holidays or whatever the hell it is.

I get on with things until it's officially "gin o'clock" and I'm booked in for a telephone catch up few drinks with my friend Frances.

We're booked in to chat for an hour. Three or four hours later and I'm waiting for a taxi at the bottom of the stairs. It doesn't arrive and I have to do the long walk to bed under my own slightly unsteady steam.

The next morning Shaun remarked on my late stagger up the stairs. So what, I think to myself but simply by way of full explanation I shrug and say "yeah Frances". All the answer needed, we do lead each other astray which is what friends are for.

Whippet Wordery - Arthur

I love my beds. During the day my favourite bed is the back of the armchair next to the hot thing on the wall. It's not always hot but when it is, boy oh boy it's cosy.

When The Family watch TV in the front room Spike and I have beds in there and a blanket each. We get a treat and then tucked in which is great.

When its "let's go to bed" time we have beds in human Mum and Dad's room and they are the best. Human Mum made us sleeping bags so that we can tuck ourselves in during the night but sometimes I wake up human Dad to do it as I know he likes to.

Sometimes human Mum stays up and shouts into the small TV, laughing and talking louder and louder while she drinks her special juice. When that happens I come back downstairs to sit with her in case she needs anything.

Phew sometimes the loud talking and laughing goes on ages, like tonight.

Day 63: Sunday 24th May 2020

Day 63 of lockdown, unless you are Dominic Cummings apparently. Further detail has come out about his little jaunt and it isn't getting any better.

He apparently was acting out of "paternal instinct" when he decided to drive his four-year-old child from London to Barnard Castle. What?

We have been sticking to the rules. People have made sacrifices, and some have been experiencing an awful time including trying to sort out childcare and grandparents not seeing their family.

You know what's going to happen now of course? People will rebel and Bank Holiday Monday will have packed beaches and cries of "well if it's good enough for him". We're all in it together remember.

But closer to home. What's this? Simon next door has come to our door and caught us lazily watching a mid-morning film! This could make me feel guilty, but it does not. I'm not a "keeping up with the Jones'" kind of person especially when it comes to being industrious on weekend domestic tasks. See earlier comment about our happily manky house.

His news is that the huge skip outside his house still has room and if we want to get rid of anything, we are to "fill our boots".

I float the notion that there are probably items in the loft, but Shaun is unconvinced. I need to work harder so in an effort to lure him to the shambles that is the attic dumping ground, I mention that we could throw out Christmas Homer.

We were given the "life-sized" plastic Homer by a friend years ago when she had retrieved him from a skip for her New Year party. He's had a good innings with us, but he was a bit battered and skanky when we got him, and Shaun has been wanting to chuck him out from day one.

The mention of our shabby Christmas "decoration" was a winning strategy and Shaun agrees. I realise that in order to clear out other crap I've effectively thrown Homer under the bus. I do feel a bit bad and feel worse when, once we'd done the deed, I notice that a Homer arm could be seen hanging over the skip and I couldn't reach to shove him out of sight.

I figure the boys won't notice.

That was wishful thinking.

The boys come home and as soon as James comes back in the door from helpfully doing the early evening dog walk, he shouts to Archie "you'll never guess what's happened, Archie". Outrage and recriminations ensue.

They're distracted for a little while by the takeaway but as soon as it's finished, they are back on about the crime against The Simpsons.

They're also now furnished with information from the web which suggests that Homer was very rare, only a "handful left in circulation rare" and £600 rare.

I point out that our specimen isn't in the best of shape. He doesn't play music, has broken legs and lost a hand from, we think, a rat gnawing on it during his original skip days.

Despite all the bluff and bluster, no-one offers to go and retrieve him, so I leave him to his skip fate. Poor Homer, the end of an era. Loft looks good though!

Week 10

Day 64: Monday 25th May 2020

Yay, it's the long-awaited Bank Holiday. It's going to be a really sunny day which would normally be a "wow event" with glowing faced chats in the office the next day including expressions such as "weren't we so lucky with the weather", "heaving at the pub" and "shame to come back to work really".

But today we are doing the alternative stay at home version and will be out in the garden with a barbecue planned for later.

I had hot-footed it to get stocked up for barbie loveliness and I was aiming to try the trick of skipping lunch so that there are only two meals in the day. It's quite enough I reckon.

No, the gang are having none of that. So, they lunch. Quite heartily as it turns out.

Therefore, by about 4:30pm when I make noises about lighting the barbecue, they all agree that they're not that hungry. What the actual fudging fudge.

I mention that I had shopped extensively, they had lunched irresponsibly while I, committed to our group activity later, had not eaten anything since Weetabix this morning.

I mention that this bank holiday was effectively going pear shaped and stomp into the house to make angry scrambled egg for self with the exotic addition of annoyed asparagus.

Shaun remarks that it makes your pee smell funny. I remark that I'll make his sodding pee more than funny. I think I remember putting "chief" at the end of my retort and every Scottish person knows that the addition of "chief" signals that things have turned serious. Shaun catches on and leaves me to make a slice of furious toast. Can you slam the toaster down? Audrey can.

The barbecue is moved to tomorrow as of course we don't have to return to work. No normal service on the horizon anytime soon so I should relax into not stressing about set plans or old-fashioned things like days of the week.

My version of "normal service" was resumed though with the Café Rules reinstated forthwith.

That'll teach you all. Freedom is wasted on you. Wasted I tell you!

New Journal Day

A new journal is a joyous affair.

Thinking of the words to come. The words representing adventures, funny things that the boys say (which happens a lot), events, some sad and importantly the mundane little bits of detail that slip from the memory, lost forever.

They are the things that bring lives to life. The lives of us as a little family can tell a story or paint a picture in time. Like the most interesting photos from the past which are not the Taj Mahal, but rather the 1969 caravan holiday, the 1974 brown Ford Cortina and the 1984 perm! History in the making.

Day 65: Tuesday 26th May 2020

We are now probably in "semi-lockdown". Just being accurate rather than in agreement with this confused situation.

We're just sticking to what appears to work and we're staying at home with a little bit less stress about inadvertent or sneaky rule breaking when walking the dogs together and going out on the bikes.

Let's try this barbecue again, shall we?

I get my work done and the fire goes on about 4:00pm. Wow, it's smoky.

Shaun exclaims that he's forgotten to put the rack in the bottom. The one that keeps the air flowing and provides the draught so that you get flames and not just smoke. I shut the doors to keep the smoke out and get on with making the salad. Poor neighbours.

The food is brilliant. Burgers, sausages and finally steak.

We have a lovely post barbecue chat and the boys turn their attention to how much the dogs will cost us over their little lifetimes. The expression "two grand per dog, easy" is uttered to which I retort pointing at the boys "fifty grand per boy, minimum". They come back in unison with an unashamed "yeah and the rest". I'm not sure that it's a life goal that should be encouraged.

James is off on his bike today to meet up with his pal Josh or Joshua as he will always be known in my mind.

I'm glad they haven't shortened James' name but if they have, I probably wouldn't get to know. One of his old games teachers used to call him J-Mac but I let him off on account of him being an Australian and therefore not used to our prickly ways.

He says he'll be back for his quiz starting at 7:30pm but inevitably he's late. I try not to worry as it's great that he's getting out to see his friend and even better if he's lost track of time. Yeah, I still worry

Tonight, it's the Tyneside Cinema Quiz for us and the topic is films from the 2000s. We're rubbish! Without James' film buff knowledge, we get a measly 14 out of a possible 45. I notice that quite a number of people on the call don't type their score into the chat so we reassure ourselves that it was outlandishly hard and people are just not fessing up.

Even for us, scoring zero in the last round is a bit rough. We blame James and his going out and about ways. Frankly irresponsible.

Day 66: Wednesday 27th May 2020

The inevitable news reports are in. Packed beaches, full car parks and generally people out and about.

Oh dear, what could possibly go wrong? Who would have thought?

Speaking of rule breaking. Today is the day that the local paper is coming to do a piece on our road safety campaign. Our little home knitted "stick to 20 signs" are getting a bit of attention and a photographer is being dispatched for the article about our campaign.

First thing in the morning before the boys are up, I cycle to the office to do a check and print off some work things. I also need to scan in some pages. I don't actually know how to do that, and Linda usually does that kind of technical thing for me. I know you need a data stick which I actually remember to take. So, all in all I'm "winning at Wednesday".

I cycle past my neighbour's to drop off my latest knitting contribution. I went big this time to give Lynn less of a job sewing them together. I also taught myself via YouTube how to make knitted flowers so this one is festooned with three. It looks really cute and I could have just kept going with it but you have to call a halt and remember it's going on a tree!

I get to the office and while wrestling my bike into the shed, the young lad from the accountants next door was just getting out of his car. This is the office neighbour who barely speaks. It took me about a year to get him to say hello so I'm not expecting much chit chat. But no. He asks how I am, how business is doing and how we are all managing. By 10 minutes in I've chatted to him more than in the 15 years of non-lockdown neighbourliness.

My Wednesday winning streak doesn't continue as the data stick doesn't work. I find another one in the office. Doesn't work. Ah well, I resort to photos of the pages which the accountant tells me later in the week are unreadable. But for now, I think I'm very smart and on top of things.

On the cycle back I spot a man taking photos. "Are you the Chronicle guy?", I ask breezily. To which he replies with much suspicion "Why? Who are you?".

Once we establish that we are supposed to be speaking to each other, he explains that when out and about doing his job he often gets dogs abuse. Who would have thought?

 He asks if I will be in a shot and I hear myself saying yes while simultaneously regretting not sticking some makeup on this morning. At least my hair is clean albeit a bit "lockdown look", made worse by having been under my bike helmet. The photographer takes about a hundred pictures, I assume in the hope that one of them won't be dreadful. As my granny would say "it'll be handy to use to keep the rats away from the bin". Or perhaps with my lockdown paunch it will be useful to pin on the fridge to repel all food raiders.

Photo shoot over, I get home to make the boys their breakfast. Ha! That sounds very glamorous, so I'll say no more and we don't need to go into the reality of the actual situation with rushed porridge and spilled coffee.

After work Archie and I venture out on the bikes. We take the short cut through the racecourse but there's an official looking hi-vis chap stopping all the traffic as we exit. He tells us (shouts at us) that the road will be closed next week. Or in his words "mind, you can't do this, you can't come through here next week. I'm just warning you. We're letting you through this week but next week? No way."

I ask why and he says that there's racing on next week and it'll be great.

Apparently, a real coup because Newcastle is the first racecourse to open up but it's a shame as it's going to be behind closed doors as it were. I'm glad we teased the good news out of him – the second person today who must be used to aggro rather than a middle-aged woman on a bike simply asking a question.

Day 67: Thursday 28th May 2020

I'm not going to write about anything today except it's my lovely friend's funeral.

We can't go as crowds and gatherings are not allowed and that extends to funeral congregations. But we have our digital log in to watch the service so that we can be there in some capacity.

I do the work that I have to get done and then change into a black dress. Seems the right thing to do

We sign in and wait, staring at the empty chapel of rest.

Despite the strangeness of the experience and the odd Internet challenge, it's a lovely service

The priest did a beautiful job, the music was obviously special and heartbreakingly romantic, and her daughter did really well with her eulogy. She broke down early on but pushed through and we were, I'm sure, all willing her to live up to her statement of "my mam wouldn't want us to be upset".

Half an hour later and we've said our goodbyes in a kind of together way. Goodbye lovely, warm, generous, funny lady. We will all miss you, and will look at wild roses and remember you.

Day 68: Friday 29th May 2020

Thank goodness for the continuing lovely glorious weather, it's making everything a lot better.

Bolstered by the culinary success of independently making bacon, James has declared that he fancies his chances making lemon meringue pie. I resist the temptation of saying anything to do with "zero to hero" and direct him to a Delia Smith recipe on the web.

Lo and behold, we actually have all of the ingredients! That rarely happens with baking as there's normally some obscure little ingredient that you don't have or it's two or five years out of date. See earlier baking cupboard audit entry for that particular horror show.

The pie is a complete success. Shaun has a little panic mid-bake when the top of the pie is looking browner than you would expect but I remind him that we had used brown sugar. I said we had all the ingredients, I didn't say they were precisely the correct ones.

Actually, while I'm on the subject, the recipe called for caster sugar and all we had was brown granulated. My only involvement had been to show James that if you put granulated sugar in the blitzer thing, hey presto it turns into caster. You don't learn that from Delia. You're welcome.

It's Thursday so it's Italian café day. We still only have two bikes between four, which in truth really means that there is my bike and then one other bike between three. No-one is getting my little gem. Isobell and I are a team.

James and Archie have a discussion about who does the outward journey and who the return. If you remember that the return is mainly up hill, how do you think the negotiations end?

Archie and I set off for the downhill easier journey.

We aim to all arrive at 1pm and Archie and I are there at 1:02pm. Very good.

At 1:23pm Shaun's car comes into view and as if the union flag paint job isn't embarrassing enough, Shaun adds to our mortification by cranking up the music. Oh dear, nothing subtle about their arrival. Archie and I consider pretending that we don't know them but of course to be allowed to sit together we have to be from the same household. Damn.

We have a lovely late lunch of pizza and panini with coca cola out of cardboard cups. Who cares if two of us are on a metal bench and two on the ground, we enjoy every second.

Shaun and Archie are going to go home in the car and via the supermarket. We have a few things on the list and Shaun declares it's too much to commit to memory so gets his phone out. A hilarious conversation ensues. James says "ah good idea, put it in notes. It's funny because Dad does this weird boomer thing of sending himself a text."

Shaun doesn't hear this and says almost simultaneously "I'll just send myself a text".

James (from IT) does a quick Helpdesk tutorial. I ask whether Shaun will find it again though, but Archie reassures me with a "don't worry Mum, I'll be there to help him." Ah bless the little boomer with his teenage carers.

On the way back on the bikes, James and I go past an ice cream van parked under the Tyne Bridge. Why not. We have a lovely ten minutes sitting on another bench looking at a different stretch of river. I say to James that this has been one of the best days and I mean it with all my heart.

It's days like this that are the real precious moments.

Day 69: Saturday 30th May 2020

Shaun and I get up at the "auld yins" time of 6:00am. I get the boys up some five hours later with the enticement of pancakes.

According to the Government guidance we could drive to somewhere like Druidge Bay and take a long walk down the beach, but we suspect there will be legions of people doing the same thing. So, after a brief chat about the new options open to us, we decide to stay at home.

The other news this morning is that from Monday we will be able to meet up in groups of 6. The number is 8 for viewers in Scotland and unlimited in Wales but within a five mile distance from your home. Now what could be clearer. I do worry for those in the border areas.

We're not going to join in with this new crowd option. The reason being is that while Johnson was announcing the great news of the "rule of 6", Professor Chris Whitty was just staring ahead with a facial expression best described as a combination of horror and resignation. I'm just doing what Chris Whitty's face says.

We have a lovely little time at home each doing their own thing and at times coming together to chat. James is busy doing his "job" on football manager and he gets a warning from the FA for shouting at the ref so I think it's fair to see he's got into it.

We have a few hands of poker later to while away the time. I win and I still don't know what I'm doing. What a result. I'm not tempted to start playing poker online though – slippery slope right there.

Day 70: Sunday 31st May 2020

I had gone to bed with an eye mask on in an attempt to stay asleep for longer than the 6:00am sunrise which beams straight into the bedroom. This should have worked but one of the damn dogs (Arthur, it's always

Arthur) does not have an eye mask and decides that daylight signals a shift to his morning bed – my bed. What a fright I get when, completely blind, I get a whippet nose in my face.

I'm eventually pushed out of the bed by the meddlesome hound at about 7:30am, not a bad lie in for me, I suppose

We get coffees, but we don't have any Father Brown episodes "in the bank". It's a real blow as it's such a nice way to start the day, a little harmless programme, notwithstanding the murders of course.

As we like our time of peace and quiet and full control of the TV, we look for another series. We come across Hannibal and feel it's similar in that there are murders, there are investigations, and it would appear that there are a couple of very clever geeks who like to solve puzzles, just like the good old Father.

Except this is not based on the character created by GK Chesterton, oh no, this is from the Silence of the Lambs fella. The murders are less "ah the unmistakable smell of cyanide" uttered over a serene and unblemished body. Oh no, they are more "her liver has been cut out, probably while she was alive, and the killer most likely ate it". This is not my thing at all.

We all take the dogs out for a walk later and to avoid the crowds on the path we walk in the field. This is a challenge in sliders and my feet are filthy a few minutes in.

Shaun discovers some "great bits of wood" that will "easily make a garden table" or "maybe a bench". What could possibly go wrong?

Shaun takes a bit longer pondering over the merits of the main two "amazing finds" and in an attempt to speed things along I stupidly utter the words "why don't we take the two pieces".

He accepts. Damn.

On lifting the heavier one of the two, he decides that he'll carry it on his head, so will take his t-shirt off and use it as a padded head support. Absolutely not!

He elects to use Archie's sweatshirt instead and Archie is absolutely furious at this re-purposing. James is left to carry the second lighter piece of tree trunk. We set off with James looking hot and embarrassed and Archie still apoplectic.

This is not embarrassing at all, as we walk past every local person who has suddenly decided that today is a great day for a walk. We look like a procession of scavengers so Archie and I hang back to try to pretend we're not with the two tree carrying weirdos. Poor James, I think as I try to placate Archie and stop the dogs running between the two groups, thus giving the game away.

The boys are going back to their Dad's today, but we manage to fit in a couple of hands of poker. Archie doesn't wear his "lucky poker hat" this time but wins the pot. He finishes the steal with a flourish of "does anyone think it's getting crowded in here? Full house!" before putting his face in the pile of chips and raining them down on his head in big handfuls. He seems to have recovered his joie de vivre.

I plan to take the boys up to their Dad's in my car on my own. One thing I do miss is a little bit of time by myself with the radio on. However, I don't even manage that as Arthur gets in followed by Spike coming along for the journey. They're going to be a pair of disappointed little dogs when they realise that we're not going anywhere exciting like the beach.

I get back home with two hot and slightly fed-up hounds but we have a drink date with next door so they'll see their doggy girlfriends which might be some compensation.

Whippet Wordery - Arthur

I hate missing out on anything. I get into trouble a lot for bombing out of the door and jumping in the car but I bloody love the car.
I got in the car today double quick and Spike came too. It was a bit rubbish and really hot. Worth a shot though because usually the car leads to exciting stuff. Not today but worth a shot. Have I said that? It's my motto. We saw the gang next door tonight. They're all girls but they're alright. Tina eats all my food, but I don't mind. Tilly is gorgeous and I think I love her but Spike says he saw her first. Pepper the puppy is a laugh and Tilly says you can be really rough with her and she doesn't even mind. I don't though because my human Mum gives me trouble and sends me inside. I tip Pepper over when human Mum isn't looking. Tilly was right, it's brilliant.

Week 11

Day 71: Monday 1st June 2020

Lockdown is eased.

People are still dying but that is being put to one side as the nation is fed up and the country will run out of money, apparently. Or rather that is the only way I can make sense of the next steps. I saw a statement on Twitter today which seems to sum it up:

The virus hasn't gone away, it's just that there is now a bed for you in intensive care.

How terrifying is that?

I tune into the daily CBI call for some reassuring words. Today, however, it is deeply depressing. It was headed up by Rain Newton-Smith who is the chief economist at the CBI and is in the group of people I like to term the "thank god, intelligent women speaking gang". But there is no reassurance today as Rain outlines her interpretation of the situation.

Firstly, the economic crisis is coming into sharper relief while we are still grappling with the health element. No reassuring notions of "Stage one: virus, sorted. Stage two: economy, lets tackle that". We all thought on day one that the threat of the actual virus would be firmly in the rear-view mirror by now. You know the sort of thing "we did our bit, we kept our head down, it blew itself out."

But that hasn't happened, has it? We are now "living with the virus" so we have to change our lives semi-permanently, permanently? Who knows?

The second thing that is deeply concerning is the scale of the economic tsunami which is building up steam. Rain was talking about the global recession which you can, wrongly, allow to wash over you in a detached way. It's hard to get a handle on the magnitude, almost too much to take in.

But when she started to talk about the UK recession, she was using words like "mass unemployment", "damaging lengths of unemployment", "1980s style recession" and "housing problems".

It's horrendous and I feel anxious for the boys. What sort of future will they have, entering the world of work in these conditions?

Shaun reassures me and says they will be fine. I make a coffee and stare at some emails.

My heart's not in it, not in it at all.

Day 72: Tuesday 2nd June 2020
Had breakfast, did some work, did my next podcast, had food, read my book, went to bed early and fell asleep watching an episode of Vera that I'd already seen.

Didn't speak to the boys and didn't go out on my bike.

What can I say?

Day 73: Wednesday 3rd June 2020
I think I may have recovered myself a bit.

It's my Dad's birthday today and the first one since he passed away. I was in a strange mood about it yesterday, dreading it actually but now that it's here it's not too bad. I tend to do that. I think about what is to come, fret about it and generally get myself in a funk. Then when the actual thing arrives, this time a difficult date, it doesn't seem so bad.

It's still not great though and by the time I'm writing this in my wee book (4:20pm) I've had three sets of tears, had a strop with myself and laid face down on my bed in the huff with the world.

I'm a bit tired as I have also been awake since 5:00am but I've got stuff done. Coaching calls, read up on a few things, got rid of some emails and published my next podcast.

I've also spoken to the boys and Shaun has been to Lidl so the house is full of food again.

Sometimes it does you good to change your surroundings and that is true of today for me. I've moved my little workstation into James' room for the rest of the week and it's brilliant. A proper desk to sit at with none of the "through traffic" that you get in the kitchen.

The dogs join me and curl up on James' bed for one of their many afternoon naps. It's lovely and peaceful with the only sound being regular "pfuffing" noises, the tell-tale sign that whippets are wrapped up, content in a blanket.

I'm very, very lucky and as I write that, the sun just breaks through the black sky. Thanks Dad, I love you too.

Day 74: Thursday 4th June 2020

Over 38,000 people have now lost their lives to the virus. And even with that startling figure people are drifting along in a kind of varied semi-lockdown.

Some are going back to work, some preparing the workplaces by doing adjustments so that customers can safely visit and spend money. There is indeed no point in going to the expense of opening if customers don't arrive willing and able to part with their dosh, in a contactless, COVID secure type of way, obvs.

I listen in to the CBI call where they have a guest who is from Mori. You know the ones? The ones who survey the people and do the election predictions, incorrectly normally but hey ho, he's our resident expert in trying to second guess what the public will do next.

So, the survey chap says a couple of interesting things. People are concerned about risk, but their perceptions are skewed. The public think that 40% of the people who get the virus are hospitalised, but the actual figure is 4%. People worry, but the same people will still smoke, eat pies, drive at speed but in those activities, they are in control, so they are less anxious about the potential consequences.

The second thing Mr Survey says, is that the credit card companies have reported people paying off credit cards. He surmised (I'm saying surmised as he didn't phrase it as a statistical and surveyed fact) that people will have discovered they save money staying in.

I would surmise that they are also nervous for the future of their jobs. Of course, the Government see the answer to this issue of job losses as retraining to have new skills. Yes, that's right you've lost your job as air crew so now you need to retrain to go into another job that also isn't there. Well, it was all cheery on the CBI call today!

That's enough of that as it is pizza Thursday! It's our fun little trip out but steely driving rain is just not what you want in June, on a bike. I mean you don't want it anytime of the year but at least in other months you don't also feel cheated and you most probably have thermals on.

Phew, we make it home after our alfresco meal and a particularly wild and wet ride home. We get straight into jammies and boil the kettle. In a very non-rock and roll fashion.

For the record, even with his new bike Shaun can't keep up with me although I did need his assistance when we hit a dead end and I had to lift my bike over a barrier. Boy she is a heavy gal, my bike.

Day 75: Friday 5th June 2020

It's Friday!

There's still a nice feeling about this, my favourite day of the week. Even though all days feel a bit the same, there's still a little deadline of 5:00pm when you can shut the laptop, gather up files and put everything off for another day.

I have a couple of tricky meetings to navigate, so it's not without its stresses but I have a telephone date with my friend Frances at 5pm. The closing of the laptop happens bang on cue at 4:50pm and I scoot downstairs and make Shaun and I Vesper Martinis.

I can't find the recipe in my journal so I make it up from memory. I think I got it a bit wrong, but it was still lovely, and I have a good old chat with Frances, happily sipping my cocktail.

We had been due to meet much later for nightcaps and biscuits and cheese, but I'd been awake since 4:00am and as I said to Frances in a message earlier in the day "I'm so tired I could greet".

So, we brought it forward. However, given that Frances had been out and bought a couple of nice cheeses, we agree to do nightcaps and cheese tomorrow night. We lead each other astray far too easily, moving conversations from "either/or" to "let's do both" with indecent but joyous haste.

Day 76: Saturday 6th June 2020

"Day 76 and it's another weekend in the Big Brother house, Audrey, again, come to the Diary Room".

"You, Audrey said at the start of the week that you would be healthy, do yoga 5 times and cycle 60 miles."

"Yes, yes, I did, and I even wrote it down."

"You also said you would not drink lots of wine."

"Did I? Yes, I think I remember that."

"So, unless you're going to do a 40 mile bike ride today and cancel your cheese and wine date with Frances, you're really going to fail aren't you?"

"Oh sod off Big Brother I can't be bothered with your self-righteous, judgmental attitude, this is not the time to worry about these things."

I take the dogs for a walk (doing it) and then Shaun and I cycle (also doing it) to Thorpes to get cable ties for the little computer on his new bike. He had a 50/50 chance of getting it right when installing it and yes, you guessed it, it's upside down. He would probably have stood a higher chance of getting it right first time if he'd read the instructions, but I find that pointing that out isn't terribly helpful nor is it well received.

After Thorpes we pedal (still doing it) to the wine shop, Carruthers and Kent, to get wine and cheese (oh no, back to not doing it again).

It's so freezing that when we get home I have a bath to warm up while Shaun takes the dogs for a walk (I'm done "doing it" for the day clearly).

I get the biscuits and cheese ready, leaving a little plate in the TV room for Shaun. How cute is that? I am a very good girlfriend.

On the menu tonight is English brie, Roquefort, mature cheddar with assorted crackers from The Fine Cheese Company. On the side I have grapes and to be very fancy also pickled cherries. The wine is a fine Italian red: Lama di Pietra Cantina Diomede from Puglia.

Wow, the wine is amazing. I thought it might be as when I asked Claire at Carruthers and Kent for a recommendation she thought for a bit, then her whole face lit up and she dashed off to get it from within the shop. I, of course, still have to stay outside as you're not allowed in to browse just now. I don't mind that at all if she keeps finding wines like this one. I have such a great chat with Frances which is evident in my bedtime of 2:30am!

We really do have infinite capacity to natter. And now that I have stopped worrying about "doing it" I feel much better.

Day 77: Sunday 7th June 2020

I actually manage to have a lie in. Which is much needed as I feel sluggish. In no way do I blame my night on the tiles (actually sofa) because it was well worth it.

Shaun and I take the dogs out for, what turns out to be a dissatisfying walk for the wee souls. The farmer is scooting around the big field in his tractor doing a bit of fast driving and what looks like some fairly ineffective harrowing.

The chances are that our dogs wouldn't run onto the field, but I don't want to take the risk. That would also be harrowing, see what I did there?!

The farmer is a well-known angry person and the last time we came across him on a dog walk, he said that if he saw them running around again he would shoot them. During that exchange I told him if he did that, I would in turn blow his bloody head off and also if he ever swore at me in front of my boys again he'd wish he had never been born. I slightly lost credibility on that last bit by rounding off my defensive tirade by telling him to fudge off out of my sight but hey ho, you can't have everything.

This little piece of interpersonal history now means that the dogs are on the leads and looking a bit sorry for themselves.

Once we are further along and away from the irate farmer, we let them off. Away they go, unleashed at last. Even though we are a decent distance away from the angry man, the dogs can cover such a lot of ground in a short space of time so I panic and shout them back. Arthur obliges straight away and stands next to Shaun like the good boy that he is. What a joke, if he had been making chase we wouldn't stand a chance of getting him back.

Spike on the other hand is determined to stay out for longer so does one of his little "protest sits" in the middle of the field. He stubbornly stares at us so we deploy the strategy used with many a toddler over the years, we walk off.

He eventually comes running which is unusual because normally when we take this reverse psychology recall procedure, he would respond by trotting at a steady but slow pace, some yards behind us, stopping if we turn around to look at him. He really is the most stubborn of hounds. But today he comes tearing down the path and in a full speed "fly past" it becomes clear he is trying to incite his brother into a chase. Arthur is having none of it. Arthur only chases on his own terms and if he thinks Spike is keen, he'll deliberately hold back. You can be the alpha dog in lots of different ways but you always have to be the alpha dog.

We get back to the field where the farmer is still zooming up and down, so I insist on getting our two on the lead again. We pass a lady with a pointer dog and a few seconds later Arthur is barking furiously. The pointer had taken off and was chasing after the tractor or to be more accurate the whirling blades at the back of the piece of farm machinery in tow.

There's a hair-raising moment when the dog looks to be within inches of the blades. Arthur is going bonkers and I'm not sure if he is picking up on me being on high alert or whether he was just bloody annoyed because a pointer was having more fun.

The dog starts to return unscathed, so we leave, dragging a now very excited Arthur behind me.

Today is "getting boys back day". Hoorah! We take two cars up to their Dads as we're going to borrow a bike for the week so that finally, we can all go out together like a little lockdown peloton. We'll need that exercise because of course we've agreed to a Sunday night takeaway.

Update: The chaps elect for a kebab which I'm less fussed about but I don't mind because I'm not going to eat much of it. When the takeaway arrives, the kebab shop had thrown in a free garlic cheese pizza. That's exactly what you need, not!

Apparently, I'm out of kilter because when I say "goodness me, we didn't need that", the gang are aghast. They all agree that the only answer to the question, "Do you want a cheesy garlic bread pizza?" is always a very fast "yes" and if it's free, well frankly "it's a no-brainer". Obvs!

Every day's a school day.

Whippet Wordery - Spike

Arthur's the boss. Everyone thinks that I must be the boss because I'm heavier and have more muscles than my brother but he's always been the top dog.

When we were born he got lots of fuss made of him because he's covered in scribbles but that just means he's a bit bonkers. Human Mum says he has scribbles inside his head and I think she might be right.

I don't mind though because he likes all the attention and he likes to be the one that everyone talks about and looks at. I like a quiet life.

The only thing that's annoying is when I want to play and he just ignores me. He can be a bit of a git like that.

Week 12

Day 78: Monday 8th June 2020

We have reached the magic week 12. Twelve weeks was, if you remember, bandied about at the start as the length of time this whole crackdown lockdown was going to last. Apparently, we would have that bally virus licked and we would be skipping off to the pub, airport or at least to see friends and family.

This is not the start of the final week. This is probably not even the beginning of the end, or the end of the beginning. Hell, who knows what it is, but I'm taking the day off.

Sounds odd doesn't it, as we're in that kind of limbo state of not really working anyway but as it's turned out, since this lockdown started, I've worked every day. Even on the days that I've logged as days off, I've been keeping an eye on my emails and I've always ended up doing one or two hours. This has meant that I've been thinking about and worrying about work the whole time. Well today I'm going to sign off and switch off.

I did the emails I needed to do yesterday, and I packed away the laptop. It was a shame to pack up my new office, also known as James' room, but I'll be back in there next week I'm sure.

The end result of this mental switching off is that I have a relaxed morning with no angst as to whether "I should be doing more," or "I should be doing new things" or "I should be supporting clients more proactively." Is it lunchtime already? I've done nothing. No. None of that.

Archie and I have porridge, and then he goes into the Devil's Room for his lessons. James appears later for a coffee and a scan at the suggested tasks that Archie and I had crafted over our breakfast. He he he!

James starts on the chores list with the hoovering remarking that it's amazing how much stuff there is to hoover up. He says that a couple of times and I could tell he wanted me to ask the obvious follow up question so I enquire, "Anything on your mind fella?" To which he asks, "Eh... Mum... eh... has the hoovering been done since I last did it?"

Now, as you know I am comfortable in my slightly minging ways. I am firm in the belief that if there is something like a dog walk or a bike ride to go on instead, then the housework can very much play second fiddle. But the answer this time was pleasingly a "yes actually, you cheeky monkey". I blame the pets! You get a whole Sheldon out of the hoover at the end of a house clean; we could knit a new cat!

After a fine feast of leftover kebab, chips and salad for lunch, Archie and I go on his PE lesson of a bike ride up to Weetslade and along the West Route of Reivers Way. Weather ok, no incidents and only a couple of tricky traffic bits to contend with. Pretty standard as Archie termed it.

The big event tonight is quiz night with a full team for the Geordie contingent. The bulk of the attendees are from London and we think they are amused by "Team Geordie" and our rubbish scores and daft clarifying questions.

We get cups of tea ready, glasses of coke, paper and pens. Shaun goes all out and pours himself a glass of Tokai. For anyone who has not had the pleasure, it's the disgusting wine made from rotten grapes and therefore is called the "Noble Rot". It's absolutely vile but Shaun likes it and can savour a bottle for ages, safe in the knowledge I'll not be going anywhere near it. So double appeal for him.

Anyway, eyes down for the quiz and the first round is on animals. We do love our weekly quiz and we've come to even enjoy the padding out statements from our self-proclaimed "Lovely Quizmaster" but even for him it was going to be a long night. This was the lead up to question one in the very first round: "Now question one was going to be hard, but I went for an easier one. Yes, I think I'll stick with the easier one. It's fine, you'll be fine. You will all be fine. Here it is, question one. It's on animals, well nearly. It's more sport to be honest but to do with animals, so here we go…". Yes, the spraffing started pretty much straight away.

We get Round One finished and actually have a good score. So much so that we excitedly get our score of 36 typed in the chat. It had been a full team effort including Archie playing a blinder with the obligatory London Underground question: which station in Zone One has none of the letters in the word Buffalo? The answer is Westminster.

I'm slightly suspicious that rather than doing schoolwork this morning Archie was really studying the underground map but for now we are not caring about that and we're riding the glory train.

We only dropped three points, one of which was "what was the Ark made from?" The answer was gopher wood. Honestly, that's not anywhere near a fact and how did they get enough gopher wood to make a vessel big enough to house every species. Actually, given the story, I think that's the least of the worries when it comes to corroborating facts.

But focus people we're onto Round Two, general ignorance. This is where it could all go very wrong.

Question one is about flags. Great. The chaps are good at vexillology. But they have a difference of opinion. Oh dear, I can feel my confidence going down. Never mind, we're all go again on the next question where Shaun remembers the name of the supermodel who advertised Wonderbras. That's his type of general knowledge. He tries to justify this "cemented in" memory by saying that it was really famous at the time. But the fact that he can remember the strap-line and the year, was frankly just a little bit sad. "Something for the Dads," I mutter and we move on.

The anagram, as normal, has us really stumped but Archie takes it on and beavers away for the next fifteen minutes. He finally exclaims that "café a rum turn" is "manufacturer". Well done Archie.

James gets the next tricky one, which usually on this type of question in the past we have only ever got about half the time: which actor was in all three films The Lion King; Hunt for Red October and Dr Strangelove? Yep, straight in there with James Earl Jones. This inspired answer is followed by various impersonations of the actor but come on people we have to focus.

We get stumped on the question asking who had "The Hood" as their arch enemy, a group from 2060. We have a bit of a chat and stick down Power Rangers, but we're not convinced. When we find out later that the answer was Thunderbirds, Shaun says, "Oh I didn't think they had an actual enemy," to which James exclaims, "Well what the hell did they do for half an hour?" Good point, well made.

That point dropped, as well as a couple more, and the scores are in. 62! Our highest score ever and we're keen to get that typed in and bask in the glory. Except we had forgotten how rubbish we are and we're mid table at best. Never mind, it's just a bit of fun (no it isn't).

We get a mention on the leader board so we take that, knowing that next week Shaun and I will be on our own and we'll be back down to the lowest of the low. We have our mid-table moment though.

Day 79: Tuesday 9th June 2020

Bolstered by yesterday's bit of head space, I'm taking today off as well. This non-working malarky really is the future.

Archie isn't getting the luxury of a day off, however, as he has a lot of work to do and one of his teachers has set work in such a way that he won't get finished until well after 4:00pm. I say that the teacher is being a bit mean but Archie says he's a "good lad". That's alright then. I don't think I ever called any of my teachers a "good lad" but then I did go to a convent.

I have a potter in the garden, finding the right positions for the two new benches made by Shaun. Remember the chunks of salvaged wood? They have finally had legs attached and Shaun has declared them "finished but rubbish". Like a number of art and DIY projects that Shaun tackles, the reality doesn't match up to the image in his head. I find a good layout and cover the "least successful" bench with plants in an attempt to cover up the patchy varnish effect. All good.

I do so much pottering that I lose track of time. So much so that I'm nearly late for our lunch date with friends. I get the buffet out, complete with white tablecloth and we're ready for the 12:30pm start. We have a great little catch up with twelve of the usual suspects and I manage to mute and unmute us at the right times. It's not that we were saying anything rude or risqué but we don't want our microphone to keep kicking in with the chuntering of 'Who's had the last prawn?' 'Pass the salt.' 'What cheese is this?' 'Are there any more crackers?' 'The damn cat is at the ham on the bench again.' etc, etc.

We get tidied up. Buffets are great fun, but they are a lot of work. One-pot stews are much easier. Archie gets back to work and James nips off on Shaun's old bike to see his friend. It's good he's keeping up with Marcus but every time he sees him in particular, he's back much later than planned. It's not until this dead certainty happens again that I remember the bike has no lights. I panic. Fully being an annoying Mum, I ring him and text him, trying to get him to come home without sounding too much of a nag.

By the third message, I reach the "come home now" stage but he rocks up before I press send. I'm so relieved to see him safe and sound. He is of course fine and had walked back on the pavement despite me letting my imagination run riot with a ton of alternative scenarios. It's important that he has some social time with friends but oh Lord, it's stressful. Stay at home, protect Mum's sanity, save family life.

Day 80: Wednesday 10th June 2020

I'm back at work. I get the laptop out but only after an episode of Father Brown, two cups of coffee, a read of my book and a chat with the soaking wet cat, returning from his night out. He gets out more than us now. Little git.

I deal with as many emails as I can and do a couple of calls. At 12 noon I get in the virtual queue for the Old Vic Theatre to get tickets for a live screening of the play Lungs. It is a long virtual queue so at lunchtime I need to handover to Archie so he can keep up the vigil of watching the little walking man signifying that we are making digital progress.

Two hours later and I am near the front with only a couple of minutes to go before I reach, I presume, a virtual box office. I tweet my progress and the Old Vic like my tweet. I figure it's all good publicity for them.

I'm at the front of the queue. Oh Lord, I'd better not cock this up.

I cock it up.

I try a few times to get through the checkout procedure but no can do. Eventually my time at the virtual box office window runs out and I am unceremoniously thrown out and hurled digitally into the street. I join the back of the queue again and now that more people have joined, I am number 15,643. Bearing in mind it took two hours to get to the front when the queue had been 1,557, I go absolutely ballistic.

I kick the radiator and burst into tears. That was so stressful, and I still don't have a damn ticket. I tweet that I'm in bother and the Old Vic helpfully answer saying that they're sure they can sort it out. Social media has come to the rescue of this old biddy.

For a bit of stress relief I join the boys in the TV room where they're playing a "shoot em up" game on the Xbox. Until this exact point in time I didn't even know we had an Xbox. The game is called Crackdown (not Lockdown) and involves you trying to catch gangsters by stealing other people's cars and driving through a city like a complete maniac, mowing down lots of innocent bystanders in the process. I put all my cycling campaigning and safe driving principles to one side and give it a go. It's worryingly addictive.

We take it in turns trying to find the bad guy, Diaz, who I discover is holed up in some sort of warehouse in the hills surrounded by henchmen and unluckily for me, barrels of fuel. I get blown up.

At least I find his headquarters pretty quickly unlike Shaun who drives around the city in his choice of vehicle, a huge truck, knocking down lamp posts and killing lots of people. He eventually ends up in the river and his avatar has to swim for the shore. I've never been confident in his driving abilities to be honest and his performance does remind me of a very stressful and argument filled trip in Crete when Shaun did the driving. I could still come out in a sweat at the thought of those mountain roads.

But enough of this, we need to organise tea. I decide to nip to Sainsbury's on the bike. James comes along with me for the exercise and also so he can watch the bikes while I'm in the shop. I get us fish for tea (haddock) and also a starter of prawn and scallops in a lobster sauce. Two bags of shopping into the bike panniers and we're back off home. It's lovely to shop one meal at a time. I feel all French.

Once we've had tea and before James goes out to visit his friend Joshua, there's a knock at the door. I jump up excitedly while Shaun is trying to act cool by saying "ooh I wonder who this can be?" I am far too excited for that kind of trickster behaviour and say "I know who it is, it's really exciting."

Shaun rolls his eyes and tries to form a phrase from two thoughts which I assume are "you've got ants in your pants" and "you can't keep a secret." But as we all know, he can't cope with two thoughts running at same time. So, what actually comes out of his mouth is "you can't keep it in your pants."

I'm so taken aback I nearly don't carry on to the door.

But of course I have to, because hoorah, it's Paddy delivering James' new birthday bike that he still doesn't know he is getting and is going to be a massive surprise. It's a month late, such is the demand for bikes now but well worth the wait.

It's matt black with gold flecks in the paintwork, a scary looking skinny seat and decent mudguards. I can just see him scooting around university with books on the back.

We naturally all have to take turns going round the block. We master the gears but that seat is going to take longer. I'm glad I have an old ladies bike!

James takes it off to see his friend Joshua with strict instructions to come home before it's too dark. He does, but I still wait up for him and have a little catch up when he appears. I'll not be able to do that when he's at Uni, but for now I can still do clucking.

Day 81: Thursday 11th June 2020

It's pizza Thursday again so brilliant. Archie and I get on with our work in the morning so we can get away early as it's due to rain in the afternoon. He gets a live lesson scheduled in for 1:30pm and I'm in two minds as I shouldn't encourage him to skip it. I encourage him to skip it.

He says he's done the homework and can dial in when we're at the café. I know it's not dialling in nowadays, showing my age there.

It's very exciting as we can now do the pizza Thursday run all on our bikes. We set off in two groups of two as it is hard to safely stick together as a four and also Shaun and James are going to the coffee place in Exhibition Park to pick up cannoli for a sweet treat after the pizza.

They've been obsessed with the idea of cannoli ever since they saw it on the menu at our little pizza place Liosi's, but the Sicilian chaps are running a reduced offering so it's currently not available. Problem solved by using the Tower Café as our pudding destination. We really are getting organised on our Thursday jaunts.

Archie and I have a nice ride into town arriving at the same time as James and Shaun. We order our pizzas and paninis and I keep a "not too subtle" eye on a group of middle-aged cyclists who are finishing up their coffees under the umbrella on the newly "back in use" picnic table. They start to put their cups in the bin so with even less subtlety, I'm over. I keep two metres away but by the same token I don't leave the orbit of the table. This prime spot will be ours.

The chaps scoff their pizzas with velocity and proclaim that they could "eat that all again." Only that morning I'd said to Shaun "you people (the males) eat so much food, constantly".

They order another pizza to share.

I had previously messaged my friend Paula to say that we were at the café as her office is two minutes walk away. She pops along to say hello. It's so lovely to see her in the flesh. So lovely in fact that I surprise myself by bursting into tears. I didn't think I'd get emotional at all, so there you go. What is it going to be like for people who haven't seen anyone?

We have a lovely catch up about work, the boys, cooking, putting on weight, that kind of thing.

We resolve to meet up next week for more chatting and hopefully no tears, but I can't guarantee that last bit.

Whippet Wordery - Spike

They went out. All out. Together.
It's weird because I thought I might like a bit
of peace and quiet for a good afternoon sleep, but I don't
like it now. My brother and me did one of our little

howly songs to make us feel better. I can hit a really high note if I warm up well.

The cat didn't seem to notice that The Family had gone. Thank goodness. He'd have had a field day if he had known.

They came back. I hadn't slept a wink either. I hope they don't start that leaving business again. I'm knackered so I was glad when it was "lets go to bed".

Day 82: Friday 12th June 2020

I've not really written much recently about the national and international crisis but that doesn't mean that it's gone away. Far from it.

The death toll in the UK continues to rise and is now over 41,000. The UK seems to have the worst record, bar the USA. All atrocious.

It would appear from rumours that the lockdown is going to be relaxed. Some people are saying it's a tactic to divert attention from or justify the actions of Dominic Cummings after his drive to Barnard Castle hit the headlines.

Meanwhile in international news, following the murder of a young black man called George Floyd in the US, there have been protests, marches, gatherings and acts of support all week, under the movement of Black Lives Matter. The galvanising tragedy has been the shocking loss of one life in the US, while the inequalities here have been reported during this crisis but not properly talked about. Apparently, people from BAME communities have a higher mortality rate from the virus. What's all that about? It's just not right, needs to be looked into and changes need to be made.

Now.

Day 83: Saturday 13th June 2020

I've decided to stop doing the count when we reach Day 100. If we had thought it was going to be this long, 83 days ago, there would have been riots. But we are where we are, and we seem to be doing OK although the long-term effects of this social exclusion are yet to be experienced in full I think.

I might retrain as a psychiatrist or with all the screen time and working from home on dining room chairs, maybe an optician or a physiotherapist.

It's a misty and damp day (dreich would be the brilliantly descriptive word) and we don't have much planned, but of course it is takeaway day. I mention that first thing in the morning and Shaun uses that as an excuse to declare that it is now officially "fat Saturday" so he can have chocolate for breakfast.

Fat Saturday continues even on the bike ride because the four of us make sure our route also takes in the café in Exhibition Park, now known to us as the "cannoli café".

We ride to the park in two groups of two again as Archie and I are going to set off early to fit in some errands on the way. The first one is a drop into the office to get rid of some confidential shredding. It's mainly address labels from the numerous online purchases which have appeared at the house in the last few weeks.

We are then off to the hardware shop Thorpes to get a watch battery for Archie's new eBay item (told you the parcels were daily). The item is, as Archie put it a "bit of bling". It's a watch which was £20 and now it's going to cost him £7.50 to get it working.

The chap at Thorpes tells Archie to come back in half an hour so we cycle along the High Street to Carruthers and Kent to get the new stock of organic Pinot Gris that they had publicised on Facebook. We also want some of their nice brie cheese. I am, again perplexed as to why I'm putting on weight each week. No idea at all, it's a complete and utter mystery.

I have a little chat with Claire and Mo to catch up with their wine shop news and to kill some time before the bling is fully battered.

We've only been away from Thorpes for about twenty minutes but we decide to "risk it for a biscuit" as our family saying goes. Archie comes back out with bling successfully working. He says that the chap had apparently said to him "that was a quick half an hour". It seemed a pointless statement as the watch was ready; this was not lost on Archie. I can only imagine the facial expression when the exchange had come to an end.

We set off for the park thinking we would get there at the same time as James and Shaun, given that we had seen them going past us when we were chatting at Carruthers and Kent. But oh no, we catch them up. There is no way Shaun can blame the bike, it's brand new. He is just slower than us. Fact.

We have cannoli, coca cola, ginger beer (me) and Fanta, sitting on a park bench and watching people walking and cycling around. As soon as they finish, the chaps say they could fancy more. I point out that they had barely two hours before had four pancakes each and that we would be getting our takeaway very soon. I get that perplexed "so" look from all of them, to which I respond by getting on my bike and setting off.

It's best not to engage and anyway the money is in my panniers.

Day 84: Sunday 14th June 2020

We're coming to the end of Week 12 and we're all still safe and sound, healthy and well. I say healthy and well but I could do better on that front so I had, at the start of the week, set myself the goal of cycling sixty miles. This means that in order to meet the target, I need to do seventeen and a half miles today.

The chaps have all agreed to come with me so the plan is that we'll go down to the Quayside, head east and try to find the elusive link part of Hadrian's Waggonway cycle path. We don't want to do what Archie and I did the last time and end up being lost in Wallsend. To give the area a bit of context when the singer Sting was asked about his hometown "would you bring up your kids in Wallsend?" he replied "I wouldn't bring up my dinner in Wallsend." It's a bit harsh but similarly it's not the kind of place that you would want to add to your cycling tour on a regular basis.

We head off at a pretty good pace, finding ourselves at quite a busy Quayside in no time at all. We didn't even have to wait for Shaun much as the way into town is ever so slightly downhill.

There's a little incident early on in the journey at the M&S traffic lights very near to home when James bumps his bike into the back of Archie's back wheel. Seems his habit of doing that has nothing to do with the brakes on Shaun's old bike. He's still at it now that he has his brand-new slick machine. In Archie's hands the old bike seems to brake fine and also is fast enough to keep up. #justsaying fellas.

Once at the river we tootle along the Quayside and spot that the Tyne Bar is open. Never missing an opportunity Shaun and James promote the idea of partaking in a little snack. It never ends does it. But I figure I could badge it as lunch and that would save me bothering when we get home.

Shaun and James elect for the gourmet hot dog and Archie, the burger and chips. Technically Shaun asked for a "surprise" which is quite simply annoying. I don't need the stress of him eyeing his "surprise" then glancing at someone else's choice and mournfully saying "well you never told me they had that". I just don't need that level of additional responsibility so I make him choose.

The food comes and they've missed off Archie's burger. Shame they hadn't missed off Shaun's hot dog otherwise I could have said that I did end up doing a surprise and it was that he was getting nothing!

I got the burger reordered but work out that we had not been charged for it in the original order. It would appear on investigation that I am the only one in our little family who would, as a default "fess up"! What's all that about?

Now don't get me wrong, had the guy behind the socially distanced kiosk apparatus been rude, I would have allowed myself a day off from my morals. I would have scored for a free burger considering it as "evens" so to speak. But he had been cheery, polite and I reckon hard working so I point out the omission. I offer to pay but he says no, it was his fault, and he was sorry again.

There, that's the way it should be. Take note little dishonest family and all customer service staff.

The chaps scoff their lunch and I pinch some chips. Shaun had said he hadn't wanted chips so I could have them all. But while I was dealing with the missing burger, he had busied himself stuffing them into his hot dog bun. He does that kind of disgusting practice. I figure a deal is a deal, so I take them back out and pinch a bit of the hot dog as well for my trouble.

We finish our snack which I think I have successfully socialised as "lunch" and off we go to find the link for Hadrian's Waggonway. Dead easy. I tell the gang that we can turn around anytime as to make up any missing miles towards the target I can just do some little additional cycling when I get home. But the chaps supportively say to keep going until I safely have the miles in the bag. Thanks fellas.

I got my sixty-mile week done, let's see if I can do it again next week without the boys to egg me on.

Week 13

Day 85: Monday 15th June 2020

Non-essential retail is going to open today so there will likely be queues everywhere and more cars on the roads… again!

At the start of this we were trying to see the positives with statements such as "let's appreciate the small things" and "isn't it lovely to be able to walk and cycle and hear the birds".

Yep, that goes out of the window as soon as Primark and Fenwicks throw open their doors. It's going to be a consumer-led recovery and of course that also means lots of cars again. Not sure if we are a confident enough little family peloton to take on busy roads on our bikes.

The deserted city centres have become racetracks for boy racers though. Just yesterday on the way back from town there was a young lad in a souped-up BMW bombing up and down Grey Street at high speed. I was waiting halfway up for the non-electric cycles to join me, when the Geordie "would be" Lewis Hamilton set off at high speed, lost control for a bit but managed to regain himself before stopping at the traffic lights.

I genuinely thought he was going to lose it and hit me, what a relief. But my calm was short lived as when the lights changed he sped off down the hill, exactly where my little family were puffing their way up.

I thanked the Lord when I saw them all reaching the lights before joining me away from the idiot. We got the hell out of there, sharpish.

I found out later that when Shaun and Archie were cycling past the driver's pal who was filming the boy racer exploits, they were having a conversation that would have been picked up on film and no doubt spoiled the production.

Archie: "I hope he hurts himself driving like that."

Shaun: "Trouble is people like that don't just hurt themselves."

Both: "What a prick."

I'm very proud of them.

Day 86: Tuesday 16th June 2020

There were indeed queues at Primark yesterday. The madness has well and truly started, and we will have:

   a. a second spike
   b. another lockdown
   c. learned nothing…

I'm minded of the time that Archie got his braces taken off his teeth. Bear with me! The orthodontist told us that he would have to wear the night-time one for much longer than we thought. Apparently, you can move teeth really easily but given half a chance they just skulk back to their original position. That's what we'll do. We'll all go back to our old habits and the "build back better" little strap line will be put in the bucket.

I start the day with a listen to Radio 4. The subject is child poverty and specifically the Government stance on not continuing the free school meal vouchers into the summer holidays. The Government minister in the hot seat was trying to say that the vouchers were only used properly, in households where there was a "functioning adult". He then used that notion to put forward the idea that this was a waste of resources as the aid wasn't reaching the children who were most in need.

What? It's not an either/or situation. Do both and if even if half the money goes to the kids then that's something isn't it?

The Government is being challenged on this issue by a lovely young footballer called Marcus Rashford, who at 22 has more integrity and leadership than the bloody lot of them. He sent an open letter urging the Work and Pensions Secretary to do the right thing and to make a difference. They said no but the power of Twitter might do wonders as the youngster has said "we're not beaten yet".

Day 87: Wednesday 17th June 2020
The U-turn has happened.

The Government has been shamed into doing the right thing and is providing school meal vouchers during the summer holidays. It had to come to a head on social media and the official story is that Johnson didn't know about the issue and now that he does, he's sorted it. But the good news is that families must be relieved, and we have a new young hero in Marcus Rashford. The news interview with him should be compulsory viewing for all ministers. And another thing, he rings his Mum every day. My teenagers, take note.

Meanwhile, I'm just working away, trying to eat healthily, be mentally positive and get a business idea going in my mind. Good luck with that last one.

It turns out to be quite a nice evening so just before 5:00pm Shaun and I go out for a bike ride. I put a couple of beers in the panniers like some sort of adult Famous Five outing and off we go to the racecourse for a bit of cycling exercise, a change of scene and a chat over a beer.

What a lovely way to spend an hour even if Shaun's mood starts off in a slightly frayed state when he couldn't get his bike lock open. Luckily it wasn't attached to anything at the time but he couldn't leave it till later, such was his level of irksomeness.

He had set it at 666 or was it 999, you can view it from either angle. I try to help by going through combinations like 667, 676, 766 but I don't get anywhere. When we get to the racecourse I set up our seated space on the grass with my bike as a kind of shield from the road. We're never sure if it's technically illegal to sit in public and quaff on a beer so we do a little hide just in case.

Shaun doesn't hide very well and compounds his suspicious look by continuing with the activity of cracking into the bike lock. He manages to get it open. Which makes you wonder a) about his dubious skills and b) the worth of the lock.

Ah well, success and a nice evening jaunt.

Day 88: Thursday 18th June 2020

Number 88. Two fat ladies at bingo which is pretty apt as I expand into that category with the increasing lockdown chub.

Ah well, as my new favourite TV auntie, Michelle Visage says, be kind to yourself and those people who have lost weight, have done yoga every day and have learned Mandarin can fudge off.

I'm saying she's my new favourite auntie but she's actually the same age as me. Never mind I'm taking on board all her bits of wisdom and her TV show is fantastic 5am viewing to make you feel like part of her extended family.

I'm actually being paid to do some work! How amazing is that. After all these weeks of helping clients but not billing them, I'm doing some actual work. I get cracking on with it but nothing will get in the way of pizza Thursday.

We had toyed with the idea of cycling to Tynemouth as a bit of a coastal change but we don't get away until after 1:30pm, Shaun has to pump his tyre up and we're not convinced the weather will hold. So all in all it doesn't take much persuasion to just plump for our favourite little Italian, Liosi's.

We have a quick cycle into town and when there, decide to avoid any of the pedestrian parts that we had got so used to using while the place was deserted. We reckon there will be more people about now that non-essential retail is open again. I have mixed emotions. On the one hand it's been lovely to have the world of consuming and growth stop and take a breather. But on the other hand, it is nice to see a bit of life in the Toon.

I get all these thoughts cycling down Grey Street when I should be daring myself to release the brake more. Just as well the boys aren't with us as I toodle down the hill at my usual old lady pace.

We get to Liosi's and what's this? People eating pasta! I'll be having some of that I think. The small menu has been extended to include more of their usual repertoire. We ring the boys for our daily catch up which is always great until the food arrives and the chaps (including Shaun) start larking about. I say goodbye and hang up. Archie texts me his usual one word: "Cold!" Absolutely.

We have a lovely lunch in our current favourite surroundings of the metal park bench eating out of a box. Brilliant.

On the way back we head to another favourite. The clothes shop, Leaf. Shaun has been harbouring suit envy from the TV series Hannibal and also, he has a voucher from me from Valentine's Day 2019. No rush there.

I stay outside with the bikes breathing in the fumes of a rusty van parked up with its engine running. The driver is not in Leaf but rather the gold pawn shop next door. I'm not rudely stereotyping there, I know that he was a customer of the gold shop because he comes out to chat to his van passenger saying "aw that gold's addictive man. I can't not get it now like."

He left his friend again, still with the engine running and lolloped (he was a big lolloper) back in to get the gold.

I look in the window of Leaf and see Shaun chatting as though he has all the time in the world. He gets a reasonable scowl from me which brings him outside and he suggests that I come into the shop and just tie the bikes together. Another scowl. No-one will take them he adds. Have you met my new lolloper friend, complete with his very own running, getaway van?

Josie, who owns Leaf, is much more sensible and says to just bring the bikes in. It's very good of her and she's rewarded with the sale of a suit for Shaun and a summer dress for me - she really knows her stuff.

We secure the purchases on top of the panniers with a selection of elastic bands and set off home.

We've had lunch out and some shopping. Almost normal that.

Day 89: Friday 19th June 2020

Bit of work. No cycle ride due to the rain. Couple of drinks over Zoom with my friend Paula. Bit of telly.

That's it.

I'm refusing to say the buzz phrase of "new normal" but that is what normal is for me today. I'll use a North East word instead, canny, today was canny.

Day 90: Saturday 20th June 2020

90 days is often quoted as the length of time it takes to make irreversible change. Like a new life habit or an exercise regime. What new life habits have I developed?

None that are great for my health I don't think. I'm not eating as well as I used to and am eating far more in some strange attempt at keeping up with the fellas. Drinking a lot more than I did and I'm not talking water here. Not going to the gym. Not doing yoga. Watching way more TV.

Yeah, all in all I am no Joe Wicks, that's for sure.

Ah well, my aim this week was to be kinder to myself in my own head and I think I've achieved that. Next week I can start on all the other crap.

We start off the day with the usual coffee and TV (see) and then take the dogs out for their morning walk. No incidents with deer, although grumpy Spike does bark at a little girl.

The girl in question was a mini dog enthusiast and she just ran up to our two canines and immediately got stuck in massaging Arthur. Not a polite or wary stroke, but rather a full-on sports massage. Arthur thought it was pretty ok and stood there enjoying the attention and only flinched every now and again when the little girl was doing more deep tissue work or poking at his ears.

The little girl turned her attention to Spike who was having none of it. She ran up to him and he sounded a warning bark right in her face. She laughed and carried on waving her arms excitedly. Oh dear. We get Mr Grumpy on the lead and he gets a few stern words.

Enter Arthur for his second round of massage therapy. Good boy.

We're off for a quick cycle ride today on what I'm terming the "deli run". First, we go to Thorpe's the general hardware shop, for a bicycle repair kit. Shaun having repaired a puncture the other day has realised how old his items are in his emergency bag. I maintain the stance that I have my phone and would just ring a big taxi for me and Isobell.

Next on the route is Carruthers and Kent for wine for this evening (see!) and some chocolate for Shaun and a surprise bar for James and Archie.

Next, off to Rehills in Jesmond for some spices. It's the best place for all things to do with making curries. Also eclectically the best place for a wide array of spirits so we are on a mission to get a bottle of bourbon for Shaun.

I queue for about ten minutes to get into Rehills as they are restricting numbers in the shop of course. Just at the point that I am nearly at the front, I realise that my purse is still in the bike panniers, round the corner with Shaun.

The chap behind me in the queue is pretty relaxed about my request to "keep my place" but when I return the new people who have arrived are not so chilled. Judging by the looks I get, they are a bit hostile to my queue jumping antics. I do what any normal person would do and stare straight ahead.

I get all the provisions and a couple of beers and a samosa each (see!). We set off for Jesmond Dene but when we get there we realise that the whole of Newcastle is in the Dene. I suggest we divert to Paddy Freemans park but the only trouble is that the journey there is "turn right and go straight up". The hill is damn near vertical.

It's quite a climb which just keeps on going and Shaun needs a breather at the top. Even with my Turbo setting I feel I need a minute before getting the beers and the samosa out. That must be calorie neutral?

We have a nice little sit on the grass with our tin of beer each and our samosa while watching a Geordie Joe Wicks putting a group through their paces. It's quite entertaining to watch while drinking and scoffing.

On the way home we go via the little Sainsbury's as I realise, we don't have anything for tea. It's one person allowed in per party and anyway one of us needs to stay with the bikes. Shaun gets the short straw and stands in the queue for 15 minutes before he's allowed in. You still don't have to wear masks in supermarkets, but it might come. About half in the queue are masked up.

Shaun comes back out after the trip round the little shop to get chicken, milk, bread, sour cream and mushrooms for our planned chicken fajitas.

No chicken.

Off he goes again to stand in the queue but the hi-viz clad security lass takes pity on him and lets him in early. We're not doing very well with this queuing business and that's how riots start. At all times we're only 72 hours away from anarchy remember but it'll be us forgetful boomers who start it up!

Whippet Wordery - Spike

Arthur loves lots of attention and lots of stroking. I can take it or leave it. Human Mum understands and she says she's not a fan of all that touching business either. Human Mum and me have our own sofa in the living room where we can sit together, all cosy but not bothering each other. Sometimes human Dad plays with me which is good and it doesn't last long as Arthur muscles in with his FOMO ways. It suits us all because after a minute I want to leave and I have to work out when it would be ok to walk away. I don't want to be rude.

As for strangers touching you. Well, that's just weird. I usually stay just out of reach but some even come after you. Again weird. A little girl did a full-on assault today so I shouted "hashtag me too". I've heard Mum say it when they've been watching films. It seemed to work.

Day 91: Sunday 21st June 2020

The death toll in the UK is now over 42,000. It's hard to take in that number. Even if, like us, you haven't been directly affected, our whole way of life has been ripped up and reset by the damn virus. Whilst we can say the words like "it makes you appreciate the small things" and "it's been great spending time with the family", in truth it's been the biggest change we've ever faced. All generations.

Sarah our next-door neighbour was saying that a friend of hers, who is a teacher, relayed the story of a conversation he'd had with his class. He had been saying to his class that we were now starting to reopen things but that the pandemic still wasn't over. One of his pupils asked, "in your experience, how long do they normally last Sir?". Nope, no idea, new to us all.

Shaun and I start the day with a little theatre production. We watch Wise Children from the Old Vic on YouTube. It was excellent and we spend a great couple of hours happily watching it and chatting with our coffees.

It's good to while away time today for a couple of big reasons. Firstly, it's Father's Day. The first one without my Dad. Secondly, the boys aren't coming back to me today as I offered to let them stay with their Dad. That seemed like the right thing to do especially as there's a Newcastle game on, which they'll enjoy together. I'm a bit sad though.

It's beautiful weather again and we fancy a walk on the beach and fish and chips at the coast. But we decide it's not a great idea because you can't let the dogs off the lead and we anticipate that the coast will be "hoaching" as the Scottish saying goes.

We're sold on this fish and chips idea, however, so elect to go to Newburn as we know of a great chippy in Throckley.

Fish and chip shop is closed.

Shaun tries to find the "good kebab shop", gets lost, finds it. Kebab shop is closed.

We find an alternative kebab shop online which is optimistically advertising "meze". We should have known better as we arrive at the industrial estate which is home to this fine establishment. Shaun goes in to order and comes back out ten minutes later with a frustrated face. Apparently, he had to repeat himself multiple times:

"Chicken kebab and chips and mixed kebab and chips please."

"Lemon chicken wrap?"

"No" ... Repeats order.

"So, mixed kebab and a wrap?"

Apparently, this went on for a few rounds until Shaun was mildly convinced that we were at least going to get something nearing our original order.

What did we get in the end?

Wraps.

"Where's the chips?" I enquire, looking at the little non-kebab and chips tin foiled clad parcels.

"Inside the wraps", sighs a defeated Shaun.

We take what we're given because the pain of trying to do it all again is just too much!

We set off to Newburn so that we can do our dog walk and have our delightful picnic. We park the car and notice that the little café is open. Oh for goodness sake. We make do with our wraps which had about four soggy chips inside. Who the hell puts chips inside the thing? Well to be fair Shaun does, as you know.

The dogs get quite a bit of my chicken or whatever the stuff was. It was an unfortunate combination of textures managing to be dry and crispy as well as slimy all at once. Quite remarkable really.

Fuelled by unidentified protein grease and white plastic wraps, we set off for our walk. With the rucksack now full of our rubbish as well as a wishful thinking, but totally unnecessary, picnic blanket and water for the dogs.

It's a lovely walk down by the river and not too busy. You have to keep an eye on Spike though because he lags behind and may do an unsupervised poo!

We spot him doing just that and Shaun goes back to pick up the issue. A couple walking by, pass the time of day by asking me "ooh have you lost one?" as I stand there swinging a dog lead with no dog in sight.

I reply "no, one is just having a comfort break," chuckling at my own little joke.

The lady then walks on but on approaching Shaun who is standing with his back to us, head bent down looking for the dog poo, she stops suddenly and shrieks. "Oh I didn't know he was the one having the comfort break."

"Oh God, no", I say "he's looking for the dog's... comfort break."

Why did I start this conversation? It's all gone weird, which is clearly the view shared by the couple as they walk away quickly, looking alarmed and perplexed.

We carry on with our walk, with a great resolve not to speak to anyone else.

We reach the best thing for the dogs – a reasonable sized wheat field for running through and playing the whippet periscope game. The game is effectively chasing each other really fast, doing chicanes round the wheat and then bouncing up above the crops for a quick look around in order to spot the other dog. It's the funniest spectator sport ever.

About halfway back on the return journey Arthur spots a cat and makes chase. The cat was clearly more like our boss cat Shelly, because after it had a short instinctive run, it realises what is happening and stops, turns around, hisses and biffs Arthur.

This manoeuvre leaves the cat and Arthur in one of those tense standoffs. I get Spike out of the way as he is perilously close to the action, but Arthur is still stuck and now shaking. He couldn't muster the courage to turn around and run but is clearly not going to take on this fierce and furious feline. He stands shaking and trying not to make eye contact.

I put my hand out get Arthur by the collar and with my other hand I stroke him to reassure him, in the hope that he would stop being terrified. He stops that right enough because now that he knows I "have his back" he launches into full attack mode. Little sod. I drag him off which is quite a chore as he keeps turning back with looks of the "could have had you" kind. Again, little sod.

Whippet Wordery – Arthur

I love chasing Spike. We have a great time but he's not as quick as me and I catch him really easily. The fields with the big grass stuff are the best. We dive straight in and set up a racetrack, with twists and turns which are like hiding places.

Sometimes I lose Spike which means I can do the "jump trick". I leap out of the grass and spot him moving about, straight back down and he's caught. It's the bestest.

Oh hold on the beach is the better I think but I get rows on the beach because of cocking my leg on things lying about. Well, why do people leave their stuff if they don't want me to make them better with my smell? On holiday I peed on a pair of trainers. The lady went ballistic and human Dad was furious. Ah well, worth a shot.

Week 14

Day 92: Monday 22nd June 2020

Boys are coming back today, hoorah!

But first I have some work to do with the knitted scarves for the trees in the village. The "20 is plenty" campaign has fairly taken off and there are thirteen trees now festooned with our handiwork.

Today we have my neighbour Lynn's grandson Miles to help us which is hilarious as he responds with gusto to my suggestion of shouting "slow down" at any driver who gets a red number on the speed indicator. Turns out to be quite effective.

He's also very funny about his new sandals. I ask if they are crocodiles "no Andrea", he says. "Audrey" corrects Lynn. She is ignored, and he continues, "they're not crocodiles, they are dinosaurs."

I ask if one is a "walk-asaurus" and the other a "run-asaurus". I get a look.

Ah the fun you can have doing word games with boys. Speaking of which I'm late. You forget how long it takes to walk anywhere with a 3 year-old. You have to stop and look at all sorts of bugs, leaves, fences and the like then shout at cars and get your sandals wound up in the wool and chat to dogs and look at the sky. Totally fab.

The fun continues when I get my two "little ones" home and we do Pete's lovely online quiz. The theme this week is "summer" and I choose a summer garden Zoom background for us to get into the spirit. It gets slightly awkward when I start to get the impression that people assume it's our actual garden. It doesn't bring us much luck, however, as our score is totally rubbish. We type it into the chat, we don't care if people badge us as thick Northerners.

New Journal Day

Another new journal in the strange year of 2020.

We've gone from a normal New Year start, to a rumour of a nasty flu, to fear that it would hit our shores, to a late lockdown, a health crisis, panic buying and now we're entering the big restart with pubs due to open after being closed for three months.

The expression that springs to mind again is that the virus hasn't gone away, it's just that there are more beds in intensive care now! We're just currently repeating weeks one and two of lockdown. I'll keep doing that until Chris Whitty smiles.

Here goes nothing, I've cracked open a new little journal. Buckle up reader.

Day 93: Tuesday 23rd June 2020

Archie and I are busy with work this morning, so we crack on. As James is now back in his room, I've been evicted from my little office. In truth he said I could stay, but a teenager needs his own space, and he doesn't get up until 10:30am, I could have done two hours of work by then!

I can't really bear the thought of going back to working in the kitchen with all the distractions and questions about the whereabouts of milk, keys, Shaun's mobile phone and the secret stash of food which I keep moving. Like a teenager I need my own space as well.

So, I set up an "office" on the windowsill in my little dressing room boudoir. I'm making it sound like some sort of variation of the red-light district in Amsterdam, but it isn't! I simply plonk my laptop on the flat surface in the bay window and start checking my emails. It's not great though. Worried about my posture Shaun sets about making me a little desk so I can sit more comfortably.

The desk wouldn't win any design prizes and my setup probably wouldn't pass a risk assessment but it's great. I can happily make myself at home. Well, an hour of polishing, hoovering and rearranging things is what I mean by making myself at home. At one point during the arranging and organising, the boys and Shaun come to see how I'm doing. Archie and Shaun start play fighting on the bed, they are quickly joined by the dogs. All having a right old laugh, in my bloody quiet space. So much for a "room of one's own" ... Virginia Woolf will be turning in her grave.

James is off to his mate's house for a visit. Based on past experience he is unlikely to be home in time for tea so rather than do the planned steak and chips I elect for a chicken pasta thing which he can heat up when he appears. True to past form he texts to ask if he can stay longer. My response is to be "be home before it's dark", to which he points out that it's summer so that's good and late. Damn!

He eventually calls to say he's sorry he's late but he's trying to get one of his friends home safely. Apparently, this friend has eaten some "dodgy chicken". Yeah right?! Would that be of the cider variety?

It would appear it was "cider related" and now they're having to get their "food poisoned" chum back to his house safely to face the music. James and his other friend do the right thing and manhandle him home and even manage to get their bikes back safe and sound. I'm relieved to see James' face at the window and him and I stay up while I finish some knitting and have a watch of the The Great British Sewing Bee. I'm aware how old that statement makes me sound!

I ask James what he's learned from today's escapades. He simply says "everyone should stop drinking at the same time". Yep, that should do it. All I add is "choose your mates well and always get each other home".

Good lads.

Day 94: Wednesday 24th June 2020
Day 94 of the time the world stopped, hunkered down and just focused on living.

But we're getting going again and our learned and esteemed leader has spoken, so that'll be fine.

Not happy to take the summary from the morning news nor the interpretations that I've seen on emails this morning, I decide to watch the briefing from last night. I need to see Professor Chris Whitty's face, to see if during or just after Johnson's blurb, the sensible grown-up medical man is rolling his eyes or not. It's also useful to listen to his answers to the questions from the various journalists taking their turn on the TV screen.

As an aside, the TV screen that the question asking journalists are being screened from is like the one we used to have in school. You know the type, a big, old telly on a trolley. It gets wheeled into the old-fashioned briefing room just for the half hour and then presumably wheeled off elsewhere so that Johnson's various children can watch Peppa Pig (it was Picture Box in our day. Creepy music that Picture Box).

As suspected Chris Whitty has not done a reversal of his advice and it is not now suddenly a one metre rule. "No", he says quietly and firmly explaining to the Sky journalist that the two-metre rule is very much still in place except where it proves to be impossible and then if you're going to compromise on distance you need to do other things such as masks, screens etc, but never ever, ever be under one metre.

But of course, it's out now and already being called the one metre rule. I don't think the little handle of "one metre plus" is going to cut it but what the fudge do I know!

Our leader is continually mentioning how brilliantly the Great British Public has responded and how they can be relied upon to act correctly. What could possibly go wrong ...

We're going to keep doing what we've been doing so far. Oh except Shaun has a new hobby emerging, which of course is burning a hole in his brain so he has to act on it now! Now!

Therefore, Archie and I are watching this daily briefing on our own with our little tuna sandwiches for lunch because Shaun and James have cycled into town to do the now very, very urgent job of buying a banjo!

This is the new urgent hobby and it has to start NOW.

On his way out I ask if he was going to the shops as we need milk (always, we always need milk) and fajita wraps so we can have the left-over filling for tea along with the left-over pasta. A full left-over extravaganza is the plan which is very rare in this house. The promised steak and chips will need to wait another night as I'm off to see my friend Paula for a glass of wine and a much needed catch up in her garden.

"Yes, yes" says Shaun, "I'll go to the supermarket in the car when I get back".

Off he goes, the would-be cycling banjo player of old Gosforth town. I give him this new name for two reasons. Firstly, so you can conjure up the image of him returning on the bike with the banjo slung over his back. I was too late to catch the full hilarious tableau on camera unfortunately. Secondly, Shaun has mentioned a couple of times that as theatres are unlikely to open for months, if not a year, there could be a return of travelling shows. I wonder if he's trying to get ahead of the curve?

But for now he's not ahead of the curve. You see I had gone back up to my little new office and assumed he'd gone for the provisions as promised. He had not. And now I was leaving in fifteen minutes to cycle to Paula's with no tea to be had before I leave.

He dashes off with the promise that he'll be at Lidl and back "in seconds". Now, I know he's not Doctor Who, so I scoff some random things out of the fridge and set off for Paula's with yet another Shaun story to keep her amused.

"Oh yes Paula, he went out to get fajita wraps and milk and came back with a sodding banjo like some modern day COVID-19 Jack and the fudging Beanstalk."

"Yes, Paula I would very much like a rice cake with my glass of wine, that would be most delicious."

Signed, Starving from Gosforth.

Day 95: Thursday 25th June 2020

Day 95 and what should have been Day 1 of our Euro Disney trip.

Damn virus!

I try to socialise the idea that we could do pizza Thursday on Friday this week but to no effect.

The reason being is that I have a meeting at 2:00pm and Archie has a live lesson which doesn't finish until 1:35pm.

"But it's pizza Thursday". This is enough of an impassioned appeal for me to decide to move my meeting and we work out that even with Archie's lesson we'll have enough time to get ordered before the café calls last orders.

We may even work it that we don't have enough time for this new "tradition" of a second round of pizza. That'll have to stop.

Archie and I are all ready to leave and end up (predictably) waiting for Shaun and James. We suggest that we just set off and see them down there.

The two groups of two is still the best idea as it's hard to get the full four peloton over roundabouts and passed lights. I'm never sure if the third and fourth cyclist would even look at the junction.

We get into town at our usual quick pace and by the time we get to the Quayside we realise that it's absolutely heaving. It's like bloody Glastonbury with people wandering around with pints of lager in plastic pint glasses.

There's going to be a terrible upsurge in single use plastics as a consequence of this I find myself thinking as we cycle past the crowds ... hold on that's not what I should be thinking at this point. I'm cycling past crowds of people all enjoying the sunshine as if there's no such thing as sunburn and sitting together as if there's no virus. The Great British Public, they never let you down!

We get past the crowds and continue our cycle along the Quayside unhindered. A few weeks ago this was a busy little section. When people were only allowed out for one bit of exercise they were damn well going to use it. Now that they can exercise as much as they want, they're sitting on benches outside a closed Wetherspoons drinking crap lager out of a plastic cup.

Stay alert, protect the NHS, save lives!

We get to the safe sanctuary of Liosi's and I realise the flaw in the "we will just leave before you plan". Shaun will take ages and we don't know what they want so we can't even order.

Not to worry. Archie and I have a nice little chat and spend time applying suntan lotion and hand sanitiser, everyday essentials.

The chaps arrive and we have a lovely pizza and pasta late lunch, complete with a beer. Not in a plastic cup.

When the issue of the extra bonus pizza to share comes up my resolve dissolves. Of course, I say "go on then".

Well, we should have been in Disney and no doubt we would have been eating our own body weight in carbs had we been there.

Day 96: Friday 26th June 2020

Only a few more days before I can stop the day count.

It seems apt that I do stop because we have definitely shifted from a mindset of "lockdown and risk avoidance" to more of a "live with and manage the risk" situation.

We will just need to press on and make the most of it but only doing things if we manage the risk and keep going with the common sense actions like washing hands properly. I'm still planning my t-shirt with "what would Chris Whitty do?" printed on it.

Today I have a day off. A day to spend quality time with the boys ... except they're going to see their mates.

I'm phrasing it like that for dramatic and empathic effect but in truth I'm pleased. They need to have social time with their friends. Who knows what the effects of all this will be on teenagers. It's bad enough at our age when time goes by so quickly. We can see good friends once every couple of months and nothing much will have happened in between, but a couple of months is a lifetime for a teenager! Hell I've even started doing the old person thing of being surprised that "it's Christmas again", so another few weeks won't make much difference to me.

I do manage to squeeze in a bit of quality time with James in the morning, weeding the front drive together. I know how to create memories!

But they're off, James on his bike and Archie on the Metro. I try not to overcluck with questions like "have you got your mask" and "you won't ride your bike on the pavement" as well as the obligatory and futile statements of "be careful" and "watch what you're doing".

I do sneak in "steak and chips for tea" and "it'll be ready at 6".

Mental note to self that one works. They're both back on the allotted hour, ready to get their long-awaited steak tea. You don't get that at Disney. Actually, this time we were booked on a deluxe meal package so we were due to be eating at the Ratatouille restaurant so yes we probably would get that.

Let's not think about it. We are safe and well and happy and safe and grateful.

Day 97: Saturday 27th June 2020

Day 97 and it's officially been earmarked as Disney Day

We have each picked a Disney film and we're going to get through them in one sitting. Well with food breaks and comfort breaks, obviously. All while wearing some sort of Disney paraphernalia.

Speaking of food, which they constantly do and I, in turn, constantly write about, the order for breakfast is pancakes and for tea, Thai takeaway with other things in between including popcorn.

I set about making the pancake batter complete with Mickey Mouse ears perched on my head. Archie comes down and immediately goes back up to his room to retrieve his blue Disney hat. We look the part that's for sure. If I'd been more organised we could have done a character breakfast. Mental note to self, have a look for an adult sized princess dress.

The full pancake production gets underway. But what's this?

Shaun is distracted because he has a new hole burning in his head to do with his new and most important bestest hobby ever, his banjo. You see apparently some sort of bit on the banjo is three quarters of an inch and for a beginner it should only be one quarter of an inch, something like that.

So rather than take it apart and do it himself he's found someone who has a shop in Tynemouth and they will do it. Seems sensible but of course it has to be done today, now, immediately!

What? It's 12:30pm and we'll never get the films in, especially as we have the live theatre show at 8pm. The one that nearly gave me a heart attack/ breakdown trying to get the tickets.

So all in all we have four planned events today pancakes, Disney film marathon, takeaway and a play. But oh no, driving to flipping Tynemouth with a sodding banjo is more important. Apparently.

Shaun says it will be quicker if he just leaves now and doesn't do the breakfast dishes. My day is just getting better and better. Off he goes with the promise of being home by 2pm at the latest.

He gets back at three!

But we can't be grumpy with him because he's had quite a time of it.

Apparently, the guy in the shop said his banjo was "unplayable", "really shit", "not even worth £10", "a disgrace and embarrassment to banjo sellers" and in his extensive experience, the worst banjo he had every seen in his entire career, ever!

You get the picture.

Prompted by this "review" of his new toy Shaun decides the hole in his brain will just burn right through unless he sorts it out. Now! So, he leaves the shop having agreed that the disgusted shopkeeper will find him a second hand one (presumably after he's had a shower as he feels so violated) and sets off into Newcastle to get his money back from the banjo charlatan.

He gets his money back but only after the banjo shyster tries to argue that it's fine and perfectly playable.

So, to summarise. Shaun has had a busy few days on the banjo trail and now still cannot play and has… no banjo!

I feel as though we've all been through a trauma and I'm glad it's over for now. We decide to extend Disney over to Sunday so we have time for two films today and two tomorrow. I pour Shaun a bourbon and Archie does a great job in providing us with popcorn, both salted and sweet.

We're all set, we are Disney a-go-go. My film choice is Frozen which I've managed to never see. This needs rectified. I do have a lovely memory of the music being played during the Frozen themed fireworks on our first trip to Euro Disney. I get a bit tearful at firework displays. One of my little things that I know about myself. What I didn't know though was that even the music starting in the film would bring about a flood of emotion. Yes, there are tears. And we're only a few minutes in! On the first film. I blame the banjo stress.

We all thoroughly enjoy the film and it's lovely to watch something new.

But it's also great to revisit a classic and James' choice is the amazing Beauty and the Beast, the original of course.

Two films under our belt and we now turn our attention to the Thai takeaway. We're a bit later getting it ordered which means we've hit Saturday takeaway rush hour. This means that by the time it comes we are nearly ready for the Old Vic theatre performance of the play Lungs.

We log on and wait. The Old Vic keep putting a message up saying that the performance will start when everyone has logged in. I'm guessing that given the dire financial straits of theatres, even The Old Vic can't afford to issue a refund if Giles from Gloucester is struggling to use Zoom.

It starts at 8:30pm and whilst it didn't dampen my fond memories of seeing it live last year, it wasn't as good. I think for two reasons.

Firstly, the camera kept panning into the actors' faces which stops it being a "stage experience". If I wanted to watch a film I would have done just that. This was compounded because they were doing "stage acting", you know that kind of strutty about acting with sturdy facial expressions and extra diction effort. Technical thespian terms all of those!

Second reason is there was no audience reaction. I didn't expect any from the screen on account of there being no audience, but there was none from the small crowd in the living room next to me. When I saw it at the theatre, all the females in attendance found parts of it very funny. When the character played by Claire Foy was getting neurotic, we knew that her husband was the main cause. Cue the female solidarity laughing. And then when she challenged her husband and he stared straight ahead and she said "you're buffering again", the female contingent brought the house down.

Shaun said that he just found her "annoying". Talk about gender bias.

So, I laughed into the void, Shaun stared straight ahead (ironically buffering), James politely said he enjoyed it and Archie tucked into his curry, avoiding any commentary.

I need more female company.

Day 98: Sunday 28th June 2020

Day 2 of Disney does lockdown. Oh, that sounds like Debbie Does Dallas. Let's leave it there shall we.

Imagine if you could get locked down in a Disney park. That would be brilliant. Even if you couldn't go on the rides, you could wander about and have a picnic on pirate ships or in the castle. They'd have to have the piped music on though and you would need to be able to drive the old car around.

Anyway, we're not there so we need to make our own extra magic fun time! Oh we're back to Debbie there… let's move on.

Today we're watching Shaun's choice of Maleficent followed by Archie's pick, Wall-e.

I retell the story of Archie constantly putting on his Wall-e DVD when he was little. Which is to be expected as it is exactly what little ones do. Being able to deal with repetition is a thing you have to master with toddlers around. But Archie only watched up to the bit when Wall-e leaves earth, then would switch it off and shout "again"!

When we watched it again today, my memory came back clearly and accurately. I could pinpoint the exact moment when the switch off would happen all those years ago and all those times. It's 34 minutes in. I made a guestimate that I had seen the first 34 minutes about a hundred times and the second part, maybe two.

I enjoyed seeing the whole thing right through, it really is a great film. I couldn't help wondering though if this lockdown will turn us into the lying down versions of the humans, unable to get up while constantly staring at the screen, eating and drinking. Maybe our movie fest weekend shouldn't be repeated.

Ah what the hell, it was great and it took generations for the Wall-e humans to lose the plot.

Week 15

Day 99: Monday 29th June 2020

The country is gearing up to get back to normal. The pubs are opening this Saturday along with hairdressers.

The play parks are to remain closed which makes you wonder who is making these decisions. Are they being influenced by fund managers in London who either don't have kids or if they do, they never see them? Surely not. Surely the decisions are being informed by scientific evidence, social forecasting and economic scenario planning? Nah, it's Oliver and Saffron who, once the nanny came back from furlough, have never seen Daisy, Xavier and Bear and are now simply dying for some decent tapas and a bottle of red that they haven't had to open themselves.

So, we're launching ourselves into a "let's get back to normal" and "let's get this country moving" strategy at the same time that America is closing back up or at least the local leaders are ignoring Trump and demanding basic measures such as face masks.

Also, in this country Leicester is going back into lockdown after an infection spike which apparently has nothing to do with an outbreak at a meat processing plant.

So, what's happening in the Gosforth Fam household? The boys have gone to their Dad's for a bit and I'm working and getting paid. What a right result.

I knuckle down and do all the preparation for the week and later in the afternoon I cycle to the office to print some things off. 4-6pm is a great time to be in the office as it's my most productive time normally, no chance of me meeting anyone else and the traffic isn't enough in volume that I'll end up shouting "dickhead" at someone doing a fast, close pass.

All good and I come home when Shaun rings to say my tea is ready. Who needs a restaurant? Actually, half-way through my tea, I realise that I do. Only joking Shaun.

Not really.

Day 100: Tuesday 30th June 2020

Day 100. We've made it!!

We've got to Day 100 without getting the damn virus, running out of toilet roll, starving to death or falling out so badly that one of us leaves.

We're smashing this lockdown business.

We've "kept on buggering on" as Winston Churchill said. Although in the midst of the Black Lives Matter campaign, we have to be careful where we quote old Winston. He wasn't always completely great or rather the times in which he lived weren't pleasant, nor safe, nor bearable for large parts of the world's population.

But we've made it to the 100th day. In the world of HR and people management there is a 100 day theory which relates to someone starting a new job. The theory goes that once someone has experienced the reality of their role and the culture that they have joined, after 100 days they are "set for life". It's really hard to unravel their view of the company, nor can you easily change their perception of what is "normal".

What will our attitude be moving forward? What will we think of our cultural "norms"?

Having said all of that, like the teeth brace analogy I used earlier, we are only doing things like "appreciating family", "enjoying the small things" because we still can't fly to Spain for a cheeky week or go to the pub instead of coming home to do a jigsaw. Once the restraints are off, we'll be all crooked teethed again in no time.

How do we hold the gains? How do we take the bits that weren't working in the pre-Covid world and just don't let them back in?

And on that note, after two years of determined campaigning, we have the news that Salters Bridge in my little estate is closing to vehicle traffic and therefore the area is being opened up as a safe route for walkers, cyclists, wheelchair users, cats, dogs and otters! I know the otters don't use the bridge, but they haven't been seen in the river since the damn cars came back last year!

Maybe the city can reshape itself. Maybe 2020 will also be the turning point in how we live and we come out of this with a more enduring sense of community.

But for now, the friendly Traffic Officer at the Council has given me the bridge news and I have to keep it secret until Thursday. People think I can't keep secrets, but just watch me, I don't write it all down you know.

Oh, damn I do. It's all just between me and you though, mum's the word.

About the Author

On me: Scottish, and have lived in Newcastle for over 25 years. My two handsome and funny boys are born Geordies so I need to keep the Scottish slang alive at home. Did you know there are many Scottish words for being tired? My boys do!

On work: I run a training company, www.2macs.com, and manage actors so you don't have to. Actually, they're great and brilliant fun to work with.

On scribbling: I love to journal. It all started in earnest when Shaun and I went to the Galapagos for our joint 50th birthdays. I captured all the daft things as well as the big-ticket items like Shaun being bitten by a shark! It was a little baby but he's never forgiven me for laughing. As a diver, I used to clean out the shark tank at our local sea life centre and am pretty happy in their company.

On books: I'd like to keep writing and have lots of ideas for new books. In the meantime I'll keep journaling and see where I end up.

Contact Details

Get in touch at dogslifebooks@gmail.com to hear more about new books or to arrange a reading of extracts from this book in the Scottish/Geordie twang that is my easy listening and distinctive dialect.

Follow us on Instagram at dogslifebooks for photos of the whippets and various food disasters.